ENGLISH

IN CONTEXT

Grammar and
Usage

ENGLISH IN CONTEXT

Capitalization and Punctuation

Grammar and Usage

Reading Comprehension

Spelling

Vocabulary

Writing

SADDLEBACK
EDUCATIONAL PUBLISHING
www.sdlback.com

ISBN-13: 978-1-61651-393-1
ISBN-10: 1-61651-393-4
eBook: 978-1-60291-711-8

Printed in the United States of America
16 15 14 13 12 11   5 6 7 8 9 10

CONTENTS

INTRODUCTION

Grammar is a very old field of study. Did you know that the sentence was first divided into subject and verb by the famed Greek philosopher, Plato? That was about 2,400 years ago! Ever since then, people all over the world have found it worthwhile to study the structure of words and sentences. Why? Because competence in speaking and writing is the hallmark of all educated people.

Grammar counts. Every time you speak or write a sentence, your mind is choosing words from the eight parts of speech: nouns, pronouns, verbs, adverbs, adjectives, prepositions, conjunctions, and interjections. Studying these different kinds of words—and the basic patterns of English sentences—steadily develops the skills and concepts you need to communicate effectively.

The exercises in this worktext provide a fundamental introduction and review of the rules that govern Standard English. *Usage Notes* are included throughout the text to reinforce the skills you already have and to alert you to common problem areas. We wish you every success as you travel farther along the road to mastery of language skills!

SENTENCES

FOR HELP WITH THIS UNIT, SEE THE REFERENCE GUIDE, RULES 1–3.

UNIT 1

1 — THE SENTENCE: A COMPLETE THOUGHT

A *sentence* is a complete written or spoken thought. To express a complete thought, a sentence must have two parts. One part is the *subject*. It tells who or what the sentence is about. The other part is the *predicate*. it says something about the subject.

The pirates	opened the treasure chest.
SUBJECT	**PREDICATE**
(Who?)	(What did they do?)

A

Read the groups of words listed below. If the word group is a sentence, write *S*. If it is not a sentence, decide what part of the complete thought is missing. Write *NS* for no subject or *NP* for no predicate.

1. _____ Blackbeard the pirate sailed the seas.

2. _____ His band of wild and dangerous men.

3. _____ Roamed the coastline on their sailing ship.

4. _____ His beard was as black as midnight.

5. _____ It reached to his waist.

6. _____ Boarded the boat.

7. _____ Blackbeard died in battle.

B

Add words to make complete sentences. Be sure your sentences begin with a capital letter and end with a period.

1. The stormy sea _____
   (What did it do?)

2. _____ swam for shore
   (Who or what did it?)

3. The storm _____
   (What did it do?)

4. _____ disappeared forever
   (Who or what did it?)

5. Today, ships in the area _____
   (What do they do?)

C

Notice that the word groups below already have a subject and verb. Add more words to make a complete thought.

DON'T FORGET!

A sentence must contain a subject and a predicate.

1. Sam likes _____

   _____.

2. The night sky looks _____.

3. Becky only wears _____.

4. Most people fear _____.

5. This party seems _____.

2 — SUBJECTS AND PREDICATES

The *subject* of a sentence tells who or what the sentence is about. The *predicate* tells what the subject does or is.

Advertisements	sell products.
SUBJECT	PREDICATE
(What?)	(What does it do?)

A

Underline the subject in each sentence.

1. The basketball star sells shoes.

2. I see him on television.

3. He wears Marvelo Star-Jumpers.

4. The shoes are red and gold.

5. He can jump very high.

6. Maybe I should buy the shoes.

B

Add a subject or a predicate to complete each sentence. Start the sentence with a capital letter and end it with a period.

1. _____ jumps high without fancy shoes.

2. _____ hurt my feet.

3. My favorite shoe store _____

4. No one on my team _____

C

Underline the predicate in each sentence.

1. I love the commercial with the talking dog.

2. He tells about Crispo Chips.

3. Real dogs can't talk.

4. Crispo Chips taste terrible.

5. Most people won't like the chips.

6. They will like the ad much better.

HAVE YOU NOTICED?

Usually, the subject comes *before* the predicate in a sentence.

D

Write three statements about an ad or TV commercial you like.

1. _____

   _____

2. _____

   _____

3. _____

   _____

Now use the following checklist to make sure the sentences you wrote are complete.

#1	#2	#3	
☐	☐	☐	has a subject
☐	☐	☐	has a predicate
☐	☐	☐	expresses a complete thought
☐	☐	☐	begins with a capital letter
☐	☐	☐	ends with a period

3 · FOUR KINDS OF SENTENCES

DECLARATIVE, INTERROGATIVE, IMPERATIVE, EXCLAMATORY

There are four kinds of sentences. Most often you will write *declarative* sentences. A declarative sentence *tells* something. It ends with a period. Right now, you are reading declarative sentences. Like all sentences, the declarative sentence has two main parts—a subject and a predicate. Although the subject usually comes first in a declarative sentence, sometimes it follows the predicate.

A

Form declarative sentences by matching each subject or predicate with a rhyming predicate or subject. Draw a line to connect the sentence parts.

1. Kim and Andy
2. On the roof sat
3. Five-year-old Ruth
4. Toward me ran
5. Popcorn the Clown
6. Upon my nose fell

a. just lost her tooth.
b. my good friend Jan.
c. wears a painted frown.
d. a big black cat.
e. both bought candy.
f. a most horrible smell.

B

Read the word groups below. Add words and punctuation to make complete sentences.

1. Weather forecasters noticed a warm ocean current

_____

2. they called the strange effect El Niño.

_____

3. Heavy winter rains in California.

_____

4. Tornadoes in Florida.

_____

5. Affects climate around the world.

_____

An *interrogative* sentence asks a question. It always ends with a question mark (?). An *imperative* sentence gives a command or makes a request. It ends with either a period or an exclamation point (!). An *exclamatory* sentence shows strong feeling. It always ends with an exclamation point.

C

Read the sentences. Write *D* for declarative, *INT* for interrogative, *IMP* for imperative, or *E* for exclamatory.

1. _____ Do you dream of visiting Jamaica?

2. _____ Wow, I sure do!

3. _____ They say it's the land of carefree living.

4. _____ What do Jamaican farmers grow?

5. _____ Many grow sugar and bananas.

6. _____ Take a trip to Jamaica.

D

Think about a place you would like to visit. Write one sentence of each kind about the place. Then label each sentence *declarative*, *interrogative*, *imperative*, or *exclamatory*.

1. _____

_____   _____

2. _____

_____   _____

3. _____

_____   _____

4. _____

_____   _____

A Write a letter to match each word with its description.

1. ____ **sentence**

2. ____ **subject**

3. ____ **predicate**

4. ____ **capital letter**

5. ____ **period, question mark, exclamation point**

    a. end-of-sentence punctuation

    b. a complete thought

    c. always starts a sentence

    d. names who or what the sentence is about

    e. tells something about the subject

B

Identify each group of words by one of the codes in the box.

NS = not a sentence	**D** = declarative sentence
INT = interrogative sentence	**IMP** = imperative sentence
E = exclamatory sentence	

1. _____ How did your state get its name?

2. _____ Maryland was named after an English queen.

3. _____ Many state names are Native American words.

4. _____ Named after George Washington.

5. _____ Look up your state name in an almanac.

6. _____ That is amazing!

C Use each group of words in a complete sentence. Write one *statement*, one *question*, one *command*, and one *exclamation*. Label each of your sentences.

1. a large purple object

_____

_____

_____   _____

2. makes strange noises

_____

_____

_____   _____

3. most zoo animals

_____

_____

_____   _____

4. you and all your friends

_____

_____

_____   _____

NOUNS

FOR HELP WITH THIS UNIT, SEE THE REFERENCE GUIDE, RULES 4–11.

UNIT
2

4 — RECOGNIZING NOUNS

A noun is a word that names a *person*, *place*, or *thing*. "Thing" is a broad term. A thing can be an object, like a chair. It can be a feeling, like fear. It can be a quality, like goodness.

A

Write *person, place,* or *thing* to identify each noun.

1. hamburger _____

2. menu _____

3. hunger _____

4. Chicago _____

5. city _____

6. customer _____

7. Bob _____

8. tablecloth _____

B

Circle 17 nouns in the paragraph.

Most people have heard the saying, "as strong as an oak." Why is that tree such a symbol of sturdiness and strength? One reason might be that the oak lives a very long time—often two or three hundred years. The oak is also very large. This giant sometimes grows to a height of 150 feet and may have a trunk eight feet thick.

C

Underline only the nouns. Then write six nouns of your own.

1. telephone

2. laughter

3. Bugs Bunny

4. and

5. hospital

6. when

7. crayon

8. plump

9. excitement

10. burst

11. San Francisco

12. friendship

13. hourly

14. serious

15. magic

My nouns:

1. _____

2. _____

3. _____

4. _____

5. _____

6. _____

D

Write two example nouns in each category.

1. **person:** _____ _____

2. **place:** _____ _____

3. **thing (item):** _____ _____

4. **thing (feeling):** _____ _____

5. **thing (quality):** _____ _____

5 — ABSTRACT AND CONCRETE NOUNS

A *concrete noun* names something that you can see or touch. *Dog*, *classroom*, and *soldier* are concrete nouns. An *abstract noun* is a thought or an idea rather than an object. *Religion*, *biology*, and *pain* are abstract nouns. You can think about and describe such things, but you can't see or touch them.

A

Write *concrete* or *abstract* to describe each noun.

1. lake _____

2. holiday _____

3. sailboat _____

4. enjoyment _____

5. oar _____

6. sailor _____

7. warning _____

8. cloud _____

B

Circle the *abstract* nouns and underline the *concrete* nouns in the box. Then write two sentences using abstract nouns and two using concrete nouns.

friendship	umbrella	loyalty	patriotism	kitchen
ambition	truth	health	workman	student

SENTENCES USING ABSTRACT NOUNS:

1. _____

_____

2. _____

_____

SENTENCES USING CONCRETE NOUNS:

3. _____

_____

4. _____

_____

A *common noun* names any person, place, or thing. *Boy, building,* and *literature* are common nouns. A *proper noun* names a particular person, place, or thing. *Robert, White House,* and *"To Build a Fire"* are proper nouns. All proper nouns begin with a capital letter.

HAVE YOU NOTICED?

A noun can be more than one word.

White House
Dallas Cowboys

 A

Write *proper* or *common* on the line after each noun.

1. Park Hospital _____

2. planet _____

3. Starbucks _____

4. ice cream _____

5. Mount Hood _____

6. statue _____

7. Venus _____

8. mountain _____

B

Circle the *proper* noun in each pair.

1. I always cheer for the (team / Westhaven Hawks).

2. (School / Montclair Junior High) was closed after the storm.

3. (History 101 / History) is my favorite class.

4. (Teachers / Mr. Hall and Ms. Arnett) assign too much homework.

5. We studied (*Romeo and Juliet* / literature) in language arts class.

C

Next to each *common* noun, write a specific *proper* noun.
The first one has been done for you.

1. team *Dallas Cowboys*

2. school _____

3. teacher _____

4. holiday _____

5. state _____

6. automobile _____

7. war _____

8. month _____

1. CAPITALIZING PROPER NOUNS

Don't forget to *capitalize proper nouns*. If the proper noun is more than one word, capitalize all the important words. Short words, such as *of*, *and*, and *the*, are not capitalized. When writing titles, however, always capitalize the first and last words.

EXAMPLES: **Atlantic Ocean**   **Bob and Sid's Auto Shop**
Mr. Al Bundy   **The War of the Worlds**
Los Angeles   **Red Sky at Morning**

A

Write each proper noun on the line. Capitalize words as necessary.

1. west seattle high school _____

2. castle rock state park _____

3. united states of america _____

4. republic of china _____

5. lincoln street _____

6. *the revenge of the nerds* _____

7. *a tale of two cities* _____

B

Write 5 original sentences. Use a proper noun in each one.
Choose from sentence topics in the box.

YOUR FAVORITE:				
movie	relative	car	vacation spot	day of the week
pal	holiday	sport	pet	school subject

1. _____

2. _____

3. _____

4. _____

5. _____

2. CAPITALIZATION DEMONS

Words such as *north*, *south*, *east*, and *west* can be tricky. When the word names a place, it is a proper noun and must be capitalized. When the word gives a direction, it is not capitalized.

HOT TIP

When *the* comes before one of these words, it is usually a proper noun and should be capitalized.

the **North**   the **South**

EXAMPLES: There are still cowboys in the **West**.
Go **west** and find your dream.

Do not capitalize titles such as *aunt*, *uncle*, *mister*, and *president* unless the title is a proper noun. (That means it must name a specific person.) Hint: If the title can be replaced by a person's name, it is a proper noun and should be capitalized. If not, it is a common noun.

EXAMPLES: "My **aunt** is generous." (You would *not* say, "My Susan is generous.")
"Welcome home, **Aunt**." (You *could* say, "Welcome home, Susan."

Always capitalize a title if it is part of a name.

EXAMPLES: **Aunt** Helen, **Mrs.** Merkel, **President** Jefferson, **Professor** Parker

Circle the correct noun in each pair.

1. My (aunt / Aunt) lives in Texas just (south / South) of Fort Worth.

2. Oregon's (governor / Governor) invited tourists to visit the (pacific northwest / Pacific Northwest).

3. A fallen tree stopped traffic that was headed (east / East).

4. My (cousin / Cousin) left California to go to school in the (east / East).

5. My (great-uncle / Great Uncle) settled in the (west / West).

6. Did you know that (professor / Professor) Atkins was named (dean / Dean) of his (college / College)?

7 — SINGULAR AND PLURAL NOUNS

A *singular noun* names one person, place, or thing. A *plural noun* names more than one person, place, or thing. Most nouns are made plural by adding *s* to the singular form.

EXAMPLES: stranger, stranger**s**

Add *es* to nouns that end in *ch, sh, z, s, ss,* or *x.*

EXAMPLES: bunch, bunch**es**   ax, ax**es**   guess, guess**es**

A

Write the plural form of each noun. The first one has been done for you.

1. class ___*classes*___

2. detail _____

3. player _____

4. captain _____

5. leash _____

6. boss _____

B

Underline the singular nouns. Circle the plural nouns.

1. Aphids are tiny insects that often live on branches.

2. Some ants depend on aphids for their meals.

3. An ant will not eat an aphid.

4. Instead, the ant will protect and feed its companion.

5. The aphids produce liquid droplets that the ants eat.

6. An old saying says, "Don't bite the hand that feeds you."

7. The ants seem to understand this idea.

C

Circle the correct plural form of each noun.

1. **prize:** prizs / prizes

2. **box:** boxs / boxes

3. **inch:** inches / inchs

4. **creature:** creatures / creaturs

5. **bonus:** bonuss / bonuses

6. **theater:** theateres / theaters

PLURALS: Nouns That End in *y* 8

If the singular noun ends in *y* preceded by a *vowel*, add *s* to form the plural.

EXAMPLES: boy, bo**ys**   turkey, turke**ys**

If the singular noun ends in *y* preceded by a *consonant*, change the *y* to *i* and add *es*.

EXAMPLES: party, part**ies**   spy, sp**ies**

Proper nouns ending in *y* form the plural by adding *s*.

EXAMPLES: Sally, Sall**ys**   Grass Valley, Grass Valle**ys**

A

Write the plural form of the given noun.

1. There are four _____ (Mary) in my class.

2. The airline apologized for the many _____ (delay).

3. We passed two _____ (Center City) on our road trip.

4. The garbage can was covered with _____ (fly).

5. Eating cheesecake is one of my greatest _____ (joy).

6. The zoo recently got four new _____ (monkey).

7. The Bill of Rights promises us many _____ (liberty).

8. Martha picked a bouquet of _____ (daisy).

9. You will find _____ (Jazz Alley) in several cities.

10. That legend is nearly two _____ (century) old.

B

Write sentences using the plural form of each noun.

1. **mystery** _____

2. **key** _____

3. **loyalty** _____

4. **day** _____

9 — PLURALS: Nouns That End in *f*, *fe*, *ff*, or *o*

Some nouns that end with *f*, *fe*, or *ff* are made plural by adding *s*. Others are made plural by changing the *f* to *v* and adding es.

EXAMPLES: gul**f**, gul**fs**   scar**f**, scar**ves**

Nouns that end in *o* are made plural in two ways. When a vowel precedes *o*, the plural is formed by adding *s*. When a consonant precedes *o*, the plural is formed by adding *es*.

EXAMPLES: radi**o**, radi**os**   potat**o**, potat**oes**

Some "musical" nouns end with a consonant followed by *o*. These nouns are made plural by adding *s*.

EXAMPLES: pian**o**, pian**os**   alt**o**, alt**os**

A

Circle the correct plural form of each noun.

1. The bakery shop sells fresh (loafs / loaves) of bread.

2. The shop also sells pizzas topped with fresh (tomatos / tomatoes).

3. Their big sandwiches are called (heros / heroes).

4. The baker's specialty is a pie crust of crushed (Oreos / Oreoes).

5. He always uses very sharp (knifes / knives) to slice the bread.

6. Sometimes you can see (puffs / puves) of smoke coming from the oven.

B

Write sentences using the correct plural form of each noun.

1. **buffalo** _____

2. **kangaroo** _____

3. **thief** _____

4. **cliff** _____

A few nouns are made plural with a change of internal spelling.

EXAMPLES: m**ous**e, m**ic**e   **ma**n, m**e**n   g**oo**se, g**ee**se

Some nouns have the same form in both the singular and plural.

EXAMPLES: one **fish**, two **fish**   one **series**, two **series**

 A

Circle nouns that stay the same in the singular and plural forms.

1. moose

2. sunglasses

3. slacks

4. underwear

5. girls

6. scissors

7. earrings

8. visitors

9. jeans

10. shorts

11. politics

12. sheep

 B

Notice that the clues are singular nouns. Solve the crossword puzzle by correctly spelling the *plural* form of each noun.

ACROSS

1. gentleman

3. foot

5. child

DOWN

1. goose

2. tooth

4. ox

6. louse

The *possessive* form of a noun shows ownership or relationship.

EXAMPLES: OWNERSHIP: **Justin's** first car was a 1968 Ford.

RELATIONSHIP: **Mrs. Walker's** husband works at Stereoland.

To make a singular noun possessive, add an *apostrophe* (**'**) and an *s*.

EXAMPLES: My **friend's** left foot is bigger than her right.
The **bike's** tire is flat.

When a singular noun ends in *s*, you can make it possessive in the usual way—by adding an apostrophe and an *s*. If the possessive form sounds awkward, however, you may add *only* an apostrophe.

EXAMPLES: Mr. **Jones's** house   my blue **jeans'** zipper

A

Underline the plural nouns. Circle the possessive nouns.

The planet Mercury would be an uncomfortable place to live. The planet's daytime heat can melt lead. Mercury's nights, however, are very cold. In 1974, America's *Mariner 10* passed close to Mercury. Like other space probes, this craft's equipment included cameras. Many photographs were sent back to Earth.

B

Rewrite the nouns in possessive form.

1. **Alex** _____ shoes

2. **sister** _____ room

3. **giraffe** _____ neck

4. **worker** _____ paycheck

5. **neighbor** _____ dog

6. **Sunday** _____ weather

C

Write two sentences using possessive nouns from Part B.

1. _____

2. _____

To make a plural noun that ends in *s* possessive, add only an apostrophe.

EXAMPLES: PLURAL NOUN = **students** PLURAL POSSESSIVE = **students'** desk

Some plural nouns do not end in *s*. To make these nouns possessive, add an apostrophe and an *s* (**'s**).

EXAMPLES: PLURAL NOUN = **geese** POSSESSIVE = **geese's** honking

A

Circle each possessive noun. Write *S* or *P* to identify it as *singular* or *plural*.

1. _____ This country's most common snake is the garter snake.

2. _____ A garter snake's body has three light stripes.

3. _____ The females' bodies are usually 20 to 30 inches long.

4. _____ The males' bodies are most often shorter and thinner.

5. _____ There are several garter snake nests in the Johnsons' backyard.

6. _____ Mrs. Johnson's fear of snakes has been difficult to overcome.

B

Write the possessive form of each noun in parentheses.

I decided that my (party) _____theme would be "In the Days of Arthur." I found many books about (King Arthur) _____ _____ life. Legends say the (king) _____ sword was magical. The (sword) _____ power was mighty indeed. I shaped my (friends) _____ invitations to look like a sword. The (guests) _____ costumes were wonderful. One (boy) _____ suit was made of metal. Many of the (girls) _____ dresses were long and lovely. This (era) _____ romance and magic are fun to imagine.

A *collective noun* names a group or collection of people or things.

EXAMPLES: crowd   family   class

Collective nouns can be either singular or plural, depending on whether or not they refer to the group as a whole. If the group is considered a single unit, the noun is singular and takes a singular verb.

EXAMPLE: The **class was** reading poems by Robert Frost.

If the sentence refers to individual members of the group, the collective noun is plural and takes a plural verb.

EXAMPLE: One at a time, the ship's **crew are** arriving at the dock.

A

Write a collective noun that answers each question. *Hint:* There is a blank for each letter in the word. The first one has been done for you.

What do you call the people who:

1. play horns and drums together? *band*

2. play on the same side in a sports contest? ___ ___ ___ ___

3. watch a movie together? ___ ___ ___ ___ ___ ___ ___ ___ ___

B

Identify the form of each boldface collective noun. Write *S* for *singular* or *P* for *plural*.

1. _____ The **herd** of cows are branded one by one.

2. _____ The **orchestra** is playing next Saturday.

3. _____ The Boy Scout **troop** were individually awarded badges.

4. _____ The **jury** is presenting its verdict this afternoon.

5. _____ The **jury** are having trouble agreeing on a verdict.

A *compound noun* is made by combining two or more words into one. Some compound nouns have *hyphens* (-). Most do not. To make most compound nouns plural, change the ending in the usual way.

EXAMPLES: cupcake, cupcake**s**   great-aunt, great-aunt**s**   fireman, firem**e**n

When a compound word is made up of a noun followed by describing words, consider the *noun* as the most important word part. Add the *s* to the noun.

EXAMPLE: son-in-law, son**s**-in-law

A

Underline the correctly spelled plural compound noun.

1. doorsbell / doorbells

2. grapesfruit / grapefruits

3. toothbrushes / teethbrushes

4. maids-of-honor / maid-of-honors

B

Write the plural form of each compound noun.

1. great-uncle _____

2. raincoat _____

3. grandchild _____

4. sister-in-law _____

C

To form compound nouns, draw lines to match words from each column. Then use the plural form of each compound word in a sentence. The first one has been done for you.

1. flash   a. cloth

2. birth   b. ship

3. wash   c. bone

4. space   d. day

5. wish   e. light

1. *The explorers took flashlights into the dark cave.*

2. _____

3. _____

4. _____

5. _____

15 — SUFFIXES THAT FORM NOUNS

A *suffix* is a word part added to the end of a base word.
Some suffixes make verbs and adjectives into nouns.

EXAMPLE: govern + ment = government

A

Add one of the suffixes from the box to each base word. Write the resulting noun on the line. The first one has been done for you.

dom	ness	er	ster	y	ment	ty	ant	or

1. **honest**

   honesty

2. **kind**

   _____

3. **follow**

   _____

4. **amuse**

   _____

5. **protect**

   _____

6. **assist**

   _____

7. **free**

   _____

8. **cruel**

   _____

9. **green**

   _____

10. **direct**

    _____

11. **young**

    _____

12. **plumb**

    _____

B

Complete the sentences by adding the suffix *ment* or *ness* to the given nouns. The first one has been done for you.

1. Our apartment building is under new (manage) _*management*_ .

2. The renters wanted new (pave) _____ in the parking lot.

3. It was a much needed (improve) _____ .

4. The manager showed some (stubborn) _____ , however.

5. But he finally overcame his (pigheaded) _____ and fixed the parking lot.

3. COMMONLY CONFUSED NOUNS

USAGE NOTES

Some words are often confused. Read each pair of words in the box. Notice that the words have different spellings, meanings, and pronunciations.

---

advice (n) an opinion or recommendation
advise (v) to recommend or give an opinion

breath (n) air drawn into the lungs
breathe (v) to draw air into the lungs

conscience (n) sense of right and wrong
conscious (adj) awake and aware

lose (v) to misplace something
loose (adj) not tight or fastened down

personal (adj) having to do with an individual
personnel (n) people employed in a place

 A

Underline the word that correctly completes each sentence. *Hint:* Reading the sentence aloud may help you choose the right word.

1. Pat was (conscience / conscious) of something shiny in the pool.

2. He took a deep (breath / breathe) and dove to the bottom.

3. Some of the park (personal / personnel) saw what he found.

4. How could anyone (lose / loose) such a valuable ring?

5. Pat's (conscience / conscious) told him to find the ring's owner.

6. He saw a sad-looking girl crying over her (lose / loss).

7. Pat's (advice / advise) is to always do what's right.

B

Now write your own sentences, using three of the nouns from the box.

1. _____

2. _____

3. _____

A Complete the following statement:

A noun names a _____.

B Circle an example of each *kind* of noun.

1. **abstract noun:** book   telephone   confusion

2. **concrete noun:** roof   excitement   terror

3. **common noun:** dog   Springer spaniel   Duke

4. **proper noun:** policewoman   Officer Buckley   police station

5. **singular noun:** employer   employers   employees

6. **plural noun:** gym   gyms   Mr. Muscle's Gym

7. **possessive noun:** Bills   bills   Bill's

8. **collective noun:** orchestra   musician   violin

9. **compound noun:** rake   wheelbarrow   sprinkler

C Read the description (in parentheses) of the kind of noun that's needed. Select that noun from the box and write it on the line.

orchestra	**bridegroom's**	**bridesmaids**
bride's	**Meg Miller**	**guests'**

1. The (singular, possessive) _____ dress was white.

2. The (compound, plural) _____ wore pink silk.

3. There was less interest in the (compound, possessive, singular) _____ clothes.

4. (proper, singular) _____ was married in March.

5. The (plural, possessive) _____ invitations were mailed early.

6. An (collective, singular) _____ played at the reception.

D Circle the correctly formed *plural* noun.

1. You probably eat (sandwichs / sandwiches) quite often.

2. (Peoples / People) have been eating them since 1762.

3. John Montagu, the Earl of Sandwich, spent lots of time in English (pub / pubs).

4. He often ordered meat served between two (slices / slicees) of bread.

5. These (combinations / combinationes) of bread and meat were given his name in 1762.

6. By 1827, American (chefs / cheves) were also serving ham between bread slices.

7. Today, kitchen (knifes / knives) around the world slice bread and meat to fix John Montagu's favorite meal.

E Write the *possessive* form of each noun in parentheses.

1. (Today) _____ schedule will be different.

2. (Abe McCall) _____ uncle will be coming to speak.

3. Mr. McCall is the (governor) _____ assistant.

4. He will talk about our (cities) _____ problems.

5. The governor welcomes the (children) _____ comments.

6. Mr. McCall will take our (students) _____ ideas to the capitol.

PRONOUNS

FOR HELP WITH THIS UNIT, SEE THE REFERENCE GUIDE, RULES 12–19.

UNIT
3

16 RECOGNIZING PRONOUNS

Pronouns are often used to replace nouns in sentences. Each noun that a *personal pronoun* refers to is called the pronoun's *antecedent*.

EXAMPLE: That *dog* looks friendly. *It* seems to be smiling.
ANTECEDENT   PRONOUN

A pronoun must agree with its antecedent in number and gender. For example, if the antecedent is singular, the pronoun must be singular. If the antecedent is feminine, the pronoun must be feminine.

EXAMPLES: The *children* giggled as *they* watched the clowns.

Amy is thrifty, but *she* often gives money to charity.

A

Circle the personal pronouns. Then draw an arrow from each pronoun to its antecedent. The first one has been done for you.

1. The referee holds his arms in the air. (He) is signaling a touchdown.

2. The people in the stands go wild. They clap and cheer.

3. The kicker comes onto the field. He will try for the extra point.

4. Hurrah! The game is over, and the Bobcats have won it!

5. Now that the Bobcats have won, they are the league champions.

B

Write the personal pronoun you would use to refer to each noun. The first one has been done for you.

1. river _____*it*_____   4. Martin Luther King _____

2. Mrs. Leon _____   5. *Alice in Wonderland* _____

3. carpenters _____   6. money _____

C ⟨○──────────────────────────────────

**Replace the words in parentheses with a personal pronoun.
Remember that a pronoun must agree with its antecedent.**

1. The year 1949 was full of interesting events. (The events) _____
   changed Americans' lives.

2. Silly Putty was invented, and (Silly Putty) _____ soon became
   a favorite toy.

3. The first packaged cake mixes were sold. (Packaged cake mixes)
   _____ made baking easy.

4. President Truman made a serious announcement. (President Truman)
   _____ said the Soviet Union had developed an atomic bomb.

5. The minimum wage went way up in 1949. (The minimum wage)
   _____ rose from 45 cents to 75 cents an hour.

D ⟨○──────────────────────────────────

**Rewrite the paragraph. Avoid repetition by replacing the underlined
words with pronouns.**

The telephone is an amazing invention. The telephone has made
the world seem smaller. In 1876, Alexander Graham Bell made the
first phone call. Alexander Graham Bell phoned his assistant, Thomas
Watson. Before long, long-distance calls were common. At first, people
placed calls from city to city. Later people talked across oceans.

_____

_____

_____

_____

_____

_____

17 **PRONOUNS AS SUBJECTS**

A *pronoun* may be used as the *subject* of a sentence.

EXAMPLE: *He* hid his face behind a mask.

ONLY THESE PRONOUNS ARE USED AS SUBJECTS:						
I	**you**	**he**	**she**	**it**	**we**	**they**

Sometimes a pronoun is used with a noun as part of a *compound subject*. If the compound subject sounds strange, test your pronoun choice by reading the sentence aloud *without* the noun.

EXAMPLES: *Bonnie* and *I* signed up for the Chicago Marathon.

A

Circle the letter of the sentence with the correct subject pronoun.

1. a. We went to Mount Shasta to ski.
   b. Us went to Mount Shasta to ski.

2. a. My went up on the new ski lift.
   b. I went up on the new ski lift.

3. a. Oscar and me stayed out all day.
   b. Oscar and I stayed out all day.

4. a. Her and Chris went back to the ski lodge.
   b. She and Chris went back to the ski lodge.

5. a. They waited for us by the fire.
   b. Them waited for us by the fire.

B

Replace each subject noun in parentheses with a pronoun from the box. The first one has been done for you.

(The game of bocce) __*It*__ is similar to lawn bowling. (The Ancient Romans) _____ played the game. Even today (Italians) _____ play bocce. (Bob Vetoria) _____ is a bocce champ. (The game) _____ is not only for men. (Dora Tommasois) _____ is the best female player I've seen.

Sometimes a *pronoun* follows a *linking verb*.

EXAMPLE: The winners **were** Terry and **I.**
                 LINKING VERB   PRONOUN

Notice that you could rearrange these words to say the same thing.

EXAMPLE: Terry and **I were** the winners.

Follow a linking verb with the same pronouns you would use as subjects.

PRONOUNS USED BOTH AS SUBJECTS AND AFTER LINKING VERBS:						
I	you	he	she	it	we	they

Circle the correct pronoun for each sentence.

1. The candidates for class president were Larry and (I / me).

2. In all truth, the best candidate was (I / me).

3. I think the best campaigners are (us / we) girls.

4. The first people at the ballot box were Sally and (me / I).

5. The last person to vote that day was (him / he).

On each line, write a pronoun that refers to the boldfaced noun(s).

1. **George** had lots of money. The only person who could buy a ticket was _____.

2. **Sally** studies hard. The best students are Tim, Tony, and _____.

3. **Beth** has a great sense of humor. My funniest friend is _____.

4. **Bob** had an amazing costume. It was _____ behind the scary mask.

5. **My sister and I** have many chores. It seems the hardest workers are _____ kids.

19 PRONOUNS AS OBJECTS

Certain pronouns can substitute as the *direct object* of verbs.

EXAMPLE: Mark **drove** **me** to the party.
      VERB   OBJECT

The object form is also used when the pronoun is the *object of a preposition*.

EXAMPLE: Molly sat **between** Mark and **me**.
        PREPOSITION   OBJECT

THESE ARE OBJECT FORMS OF PRONOUNS:							
me	you	him	her	it	us	you	them

A

Underline the pronouns used as objects.

1. The principal called them together.

2. He introduced me to the students.

3. After the introduction I thanked her.

4. For a minute the students just stared at me.

5. Their stares did not frighten me, however.

6. I spoke to them for nearly an hour.

7. At the end, the students asked me questions.

Circle the object form of the pronoun.

1. Please sign (we / us) up for the table tennis tournament.

2. The number one team will be Jeff and (I / me).

3. Unfortunately, that fancy paddle belongs to (he / him).

4. The sponsors bought Brian and (her / she) new T-shirts.

Reflexive pronouns end in *self* or *selves*. They refer back to a noun or pronoun already named.

EXAMPLES: Carla did her homework ***herself***.

Wilbur ***himself*** was at fault.

They must earn the money ***themselves***.

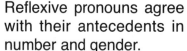
HAVE YOU NOTICED?

Reflexive pronouns agree with their antecedents in number and gender.

 A

Circle the reflexive pronouns. Draw an arrow to the nouns or pronouns they refer back to. The first one has been done for you.

1. Eric and Dustin wanted to get the old car running themselves.

2. "The engine is a mess," Eric said. "I don't think I can fix it myself."

3. "Well, this old car won't repair itself," replied Dustin.

4. "If we can't repair it ourselves, we can ask for help."

5. Eric's mother was quite a mechanic herself.

 B

Choose a reflexive pronoun from the box to complete each sentence. Make sure the pronoun agrees with its antecedent.

myself	yourself	herself	himself	itself
ourselves		yourselves		themselves

1. It was Saturday night, and I was staying home by _____.

2. "Make _____ comfortable," Mom said as she left.

3. I _____ wished I was out with my friends.

4. My best friend Laura had gotten _____ a babysitting job.

5. My two little cats looked lonely _____.

A *possessive pronoun* shows ownership or relationship. Some possessive pronouns always appear *before* nouns.

EXAMPLES: In ***his*** forecast, the weatherman called for rain.

The McGuires kept all ***their*** cars indoors.

Some possessive pronouns *cannot* be used before nouns.

EXAMPLES: Tina is glad the bike is ***hers***.

That book must be ***yours***.

A

Underline only the possessive pronoun in each sentence.

1. My friends and I have our favorite stores.

2. We buy most of our clothes downtown.

3. Other people buy theirs at the local mall.

4. Its stores stay open until 9:00 P.M.

5. What is your favorite place to shop?

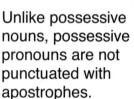

HAVE YOU NOTICED?

Unlike possessive nouns, possessive pronouns are not punctuated with apostrophes.

B

Circle the correct possessive pronouns.

1. That front row seat on the end is (my / mine).

2. I bought (my / mine) concert ticket months ago.

3. My friends bought (their / theirs) yesterday.

4. (Their / Theirs) seats are way in the back.

5. The Grimy Gophers play (their / theirs) set first.

6. We should leave (our / ours) houses by 7:00.

4. COMMONLY CONFUSED PRONOUNS

USAGE NOTES

The *possessive pronouns its, their, whose,* and *your* are often confused with contractions. Remember that there is no apostrophe in possessive pronouns.

POSSESSIVE PRONOUN	CONTRACTION
its	it's (it is)
their	they're (they are)
whose	who's (who is)
your	you're (you are)

EXAMPLES:

The tree lost *its* top in the storm.
It's time to clean up the mess.

The boys cooked for *their* parents.
They're going out for ice cream.

A

Cross out each incorrect pronoun and write it correctly on the line. The first one has been done for you.

1. In ~~you're~~ CD collection, you may have some rap music. ___*your*___

2. Rap had it's beginnings in the mid-seventies. _____

3. I know some people who's favorite music is rap. _____

4. Many rappers tell about they're life in the big cities. _____

B

Write sentences using *its, their, whose,* and *your.*

1. _____

_____

2. _____

_____

3. _____

_____

4. _____

_____

DEMONSTRATIVE PRONOUNS

Demonstrative pronouns point out *persons*, *places*, and *things*. Some demonstrative pronouns are *this*, *these*, *that*, and *those*. Notice that some are singular and some are plural.

SINGULAR: this, that   **PLURAL: these, those**

EXAMPLES: *This* is the world's biggest pizza. (SINGULAR)
            These are the world's biggest pizzas. (PLURAL)

This and *these* point out persons and things that are nearby.

That and *those* point out persons and things that are farther away.

A

Underline each demonstrative pronoun. Then write *S* or *P* to show whether the pronoun is *singular* or *plural*.

1. _____ This is a very deep swimming hole.

2. _____ That is the path to the campgrounds.

3. _____ These are my best friends, Todd and Sandy Harmon.

4. _____ "What a mess!" Mrs. March cried out. "Who did this?"

5. _____ Those are the most difficult holes on the golf course.

B

Write the correct demonstrative pronoun on the line.

1. "Did you hear _____ (these / that) noise outside?" asked Fred.

2. "_____ (Those / This) sounded like screams!" replied Fran.

3. She pointed to the door. "Lock _____ (that / those)!" she cried.

4. Fred went to all the windows. "I'm locking _____ (this / these), too!"

5. "Look at _____ (that / these)!" laughed Fran as the howling cat ran past the window.

A *relative pronoun* connects a noun or pronoun with a word group that tells more about it. The relative pronouns are *who, whom, whose, which,* and *that.*

EXAMPLE: Did you eat the sandwich *that* I left in the refrigerator?

The relative pronouns *who, whom,* and *whose* refer to people. *Who* is used as a *subject. Whom* is used as an *object. Whose* shows *ownership* or *relationship.*

EXAMPLES: I know a girl *who* wears flowers in her hair.

The candidate *whom* you voted for won the election.

The author *whose* book I read will speak to the class.

The relative pronouns *that* and *which* refer to places or things.

EXAMPLES: I must return the library book *that* I borrowed.

That dog, *which* was the one I wanted, was already sold.

Circle the relative pronoun and underline its antecedent. *Hint:* **The antecedent usually comes just *before* the relative pronoun.**

1. He is a man whose ideas are always worth hearing.

2. Do you know the kids who moved in across the street?

3. They say it's the early bird that always gets the worm.

4. The novel *Sounder*, which I've read six times, makes me cry.

5. The person whom I've brought to speak today is a U.S. senator.

Complete each sentence with a relative pronoun.

1. People _____ live in glass houses shouldn't throw stones.

2. A dog _____ chases cars is likely to get hurt.

3. That is the fellow _____ I saw at the scene of the crime.

4. Are you the careless person _____ skateboard is on the stairs?

24 — INTERROGATIVE PRONOUNS

Interrogative pronouns are used to ask questions.

what	which	who	whom	whose

Who, *whom*, and *whose* refer to people. *Who* is used as a *subject*. *Whom* is used as an *object*. *Whose* shows *ownership* or *relationship*.

EXAMPLES: **Who** is the handsome young man?

To **whom** is the letter addressed?

Whose laptop computer is this?

What and *which* refer to people, places, or things. *Which* is used when there is a choice between two or more persons, places, or things.

EXAMPLES: **What** is the matter with you today?

Which of the shirts do you plan to buy?

A

Underline each interrogative pronoun. *Hint:* **Some sentences have more than one.**

1. What happened in that room, and to whom did it happen?

2. Who was peeking through the window just now?

3. Which of the contestants won the game?

4. For whom is the crowd applauding so loudly?

5. Which is the best essay in the group, and whose is it?

B

Complete each sentence with an interrogative pronoun.
Hint: **Answers will rhyme with the last word in the question.**

1. _____ is the girl all dressed in blue?

2. To _____ in the room are you handing that broom?

3. _____ could have caused the door to slam shut?

4. _____ of the cakes is most creamy and rich?

5. _____ are these shoes?

An *indefinite pronoun* stands on its own. It does not take the place of a particular noun. Usually, its antecedent is not known.

EXAMPLES: *They* say that wisdom comes with age.

No one was around.

SINGULAR INDEFINITE PRONOUNS:					
another	anybody	anyone	anything	each	either
everybody	everyone	everything	neither	nobody	no one
nothing	one	other	somebody	someone	something

PLURAL INDEFINITE PRONOUNS:			
both	few	many	several

INDEFINITE PRONOUNS THAT MAY BE SINGULAR OR PLURAL:					
all	any	most	none	some	such

 A

Circle the indefinite pronouns. If there is no indefinite pronoun in the sentence, write *None* on the line.

1. _____ No one could argue the point.

2. _____ Some people work too hard.

3. _____ Many try, but few succeed.

4. _____ Most employees enjoy holidays.

5. _____ Nothing can stop me now!

B

Circle the indefinite pronouns.

No one knows who murdered Miss Scarlet.

Some say it was Colonel Mustard. Everyone saw

him in the study with her. Some say he had a knife in

his back pocket. All agree that something must be done.

Most feel the police should be called immediately.

5. Using Pronouns Correctly

Watch out for these common pronoun problems!

Pronoun Problem 1: Unnecessary Pronouns

Can you find the error in the following sentence?

My great-grandfather he fought in World War II.

The problem is the use of the pronoun *he*. Since the sentence already has a noun as a subject—*grandfather*—the pronoun is not needed. The sentence should read:

My great-grandfather fought in World War II.

Pronoun Problem 2: Order of Pronouns

Always put pronouns that stand for oneself (*I, me, my, mine*) after pronouns or nouns that refer to others. Avoid the "me first" problem!

EXAMPLES: Tom and *I* have the same birthday.

The clerk gave free ice cream to Grandma and **me**.

Do you believe his story or **mine**?

A

Write C or I to tell whether the pronoun in each sentence is *correct* or *incorrect*.

1. _____ The winning science project belongs to Margo and me.

2. _____ The judges they gave us a blue ribbon.

3. _____ I and Margo plan to work together again.

4. _____ Poor Ryan he had the worst project in the class.

5. _____ The volcano that he made fell apart.

B

Complete each sentence. Write a person's name in one blank and *I* or *me* in the other.

1. I think that either _____ or _____ will get the job.

2. _____ and _____ won a free trip to Hawaii!

3. The roller coaster frightened both _____ and _____.

PRONOUN PROBLEM 3: Nonstandard Forms

Use only *standard* forms of pronouns when you speak and write. The sentences in the first column have some common problems.

NONSTANDARD:	STANDARD:
Jeff was pleased with hisself.	Jeff was pleased with himself.
We fixed ourselfs snacks.	We fixed ourselves snacks.
The guests enjoyed theirselves.	The guests enjoyed themselves.

PRONOUN PROBLEM 4: Who and Whom

Who refers to the person performing an action. It is a *subject.*

Whom refers to the person receiving an action. It is an *object.*

EXAMPLES: ***Who*** is standing in the doorway?   To ***whom*** are you speaking?

 C

Circle the correct pronoun forms.

1. (Who / Whom) would you trust with your life?

2. (Who / Whom) rented that terrible video?

3. Can we repair the broken windows (ourselfs / ourselves)?

4. (Who / Whom) can I rely upon to do the job carefully?

5. The members built (themselves / theirselves) a new clubhouse.

6. For (who / whom) was this mysterious message intended?

7. Ed is the only worker (who / whom) cleans up after (himself / hisself).

D

Write one sentence using the pronoun *who* and one using *whom*.

1. _____

2. _____

A Write a letter to match each term on the left with its definition on the right.

1. _____ **personal pronoun**

2. _____ **antecedent**

3. _____ **possessive pronoun**

4. _____ **interrogative pronoun**

5. _____ **indefinite pronoun**

a. the noun or nouns that the pronoun replaces or refers to

b. a pronoun that does not replace or refer to a particular noun

c. a pronoun that shows ownership or relationship

d. a word that takes the place of a noun, group of nouns, or word group that contains nouns

e. a pronoun used to ask a question

B Underline one or more pronouns in each sentence.

1. The name "Uncle Sam" stands for the United States and its people.

2. Many believe it was first used by soldiers during the War of 1812.

3. They once stamped government wagons with the letters *U.S.*

4. People who were against the war said that stood for "Uncle Sam."

5. These people said that "Uncle Sam" was a foolish symbol.

6. Over time, however, the American people began to like him.

7. His name lost its bad meaning and came to stand for our country.

C Circle the pronoun that correctly completes each sentence.

1. (Whose / Who's) special day is the second Sunday in May?

2. Ann Jarvis, (who / whom) lived in Philadelphia, wanted to honor mothers.

3. (Her / She) worked for a law (that / this) created a national holiday.

4. It was (her / she) (who / whom) first gave out carnations on Mother's Day.

5. (I / me) honor my mother on (that / these) day, too.

6. My sister and (me / I) like to do something special for (she / her).

D Complete each item with a pronoun from the box.

he	him	himself	I	they	them	themselves
who	whom	me	that	these	which	his

1. _____ and Robert are putting on a car wash.

2. For _____ are they trying to raise money?

3. At first, Robert wanted to do all the work _____.

4. "No," said _____ friend Carl. "Let _____ help."

5. All day the two boys worked by _____.

6. No one else came along to help _____.

7. _____ made $100, _____ is a lot of money.

E Write a sentence using each of the following pronouns.

I	him	herself	who	its	someone

1. _____

2. _____

3. _____

4. _____

5. _____

6. _____

UNIT
4

VERBS

FOR HELP WITH THIS UNIT, SEE THE REFERENCE GUIDE, RULES 20–25.

26 RECOGNIZING VERBS

Every sentence must have a *verb*. An *action verb* expresses physical or mental action. A *linking verb* expresses what is or seems to be.

EXAMPLES: Mario ***ran*** up the hill at top speed. (ACTION VERB)
Mario ***is*** a marathon runner. (LINKING VERB)

Every sentence has a subject and a predicate. The verb is *always* in the predicate.

A

Circle the verb or verbs in each sentence.

1. In 1912, the *Titanic* was the world's largest, fastest ship.

2. Shipbuilders worked on it for three years.

3. The enormous *Titanic* had eight decks.

4. The White Star Line boasted about the ship's size.

5. On April 10, 1912, the first passengers and crew boarded the *Titanic*.

6. Everyone felt excited, eager, and safe.

7. The day of departure was fine and clear.

8. The ship steamed away from the dock.

9. It was leaving England and heading for New York.

10. Colonel John J. Astor and his young bride, Madeline, were among those on board.

B

Underline one or more verbs in each sentence.

1. Because the Astors were very rich, they brought diamond jewelry aboard the *Titanic*.

2. The *Titanic* crew stowed and guarded $11 million worth of jewels.

3. The night of April 14 felt and looked very cold.

4. The *Titanic* was about 1,000 miles from New York.

5. The glassy-looking sea seemed strangely still.

6. Passengers stayed off the decks and tried to keep warm.

7. The *Titanic* reached the dangerous ice fields off Newfoundland.

8. It steamed through the icebergs, avoiding them carefully.

9. The ship traveled fast, trying for a new speed record.

10. One iceberg went unnoticed, and the *Titanic* hit it at top speed.

C

Complete each sentence with a verb of your own.

1. I _____ through the airport to my gate.

2. I like to _____ by airplane.

3. I _____ it is a safe way to go.

D

Write five sentences about a trip you've taken or would like to take. Underline each verb that you use.

1. _____

2. _____

3. _____

4. _____

5. _____

An *action verb* expresses either a physical or mental action. An action verb tells what the subject is doing.

EXAMPLES: I *watched* a film about a brave young man. (PHYSICAL ACTION)

I *thought* about his story for days. (MENTAL ACTION)

A

Circle the action verb in each sentence. Write *P* if the action is *physical* or *M* if the action is *mental*.

1. _____ Joe DiMaggio started the 1941 baseball season with a hitting slump.

2. _____ He never worried, however.

3. _____ He swung at every good pitch.

4. _____ He knew that he was good.

5. _____ On June 29, 1941, Joe DiMaggio broke a record.

6. _____ He got a hit in 45 consecutive games.

7. _____ His streak finally ended on July 17.

8. _____ The record books told the story.

9. _____ For 56 games in a row, Joe DiMaggio hit successfully.

10. _____ Baseball fans remember DiMaggio as one of the greats!

B

Add an action verb (mental or physical) that tells what each subject does or did. The first one has been done for you.

1. The shaggy dog on the back porch ___*barks*___ .

2. The out-of-control delivery van _____ .

3. The school of sharks _____ .

4. On my way to school, I _____ .

5. My best friend often _____ .

Linking verbs express what is or what seems to be. They link the subject of the sentence with the predicate. The most common linking verbs are *be*, *am*, *is*, *are*, *was*, and *were*.

EXAMPLE: Max *is* our basset hound.

Other common linking verbs include *act*, *appear*, *become*, *feel*, *grow*, *look*, *remain*, *seem*, *smell*, *sound*, *stay*, and *taste*. Many of these words can also be used as action verbs.

EXAMPLES: The basset hound *looked* sad. (LINKING VERB)

The basset hound *looked* at the cat. (ACTION VERB)

A

Underline the verb in each sentence. Write *AV* for *action verb* or *LV* for *linking verb*.

1. _____ Libby seems confident about today's dog show.

2. _____ Her dog, Scout, is a beautiful poodle.

3. _____ After his shampoo, Scout smells like roses.

4. _____ Scout smells steak cooking in the kitchen.

5. _____ Scout appears to be calm and ready.

6. _____ He and the other dogs are in the ring.

7. _____ A cat suddenly appears in the doorway.

8. _____ Many of the dogs become excited.

9. _____ Only one well-behaved spaniel remains calm.

B

Fill in each blank with a linking verb.

1. The name of this book _____ *The Pearl*.

2. The team members _____ nervous.

3. In the evening, the light _____ dim.

A verb must agree in person and in number with the subject of the sentence. The following chart shows how to make a subject and regular verb agree.

	SINGULAR	PLURAL
FIRST PERSON	I *talk*	we *talk*
SECOND PERSON	you *talk*	you *talk*
THIRD PERSON	he, she, it *talks**	they *talk*

* Note that the letter *s* is added to the verb when the subject is third person singular and the verb expresses present tense.

A

Underline the verb that correctly completes each sentence.

1. The oriole (belong / belongs) to the blackbird family.

2. I (like / likes) the bird's orange and black colors.

3. You (see / sees) orioles throughout Canada and the Americas.

4. Orioles (sing / sings) in loud, musical tones.

5. They (weave / weaves) graceful, hanging nests.

6. Sometimes I (see / sees) orioles in my backyard.

B

Cross out the incorrect verbs. Write the correct verbs above them. *Hint:* **One sentence has more than one verb error.**

1. Imagines that you lives in the 1940s.

2. You and your friends enjoys big bands like Benny Goodman and Duke Ellington.

3. These big bands tours the country.

4. You waits in long lines for tickets to every show.

Some verbs are *irregular*. In order to agree with their subject, they change form by changing spelling. As an example, the chart below shows the forms of the irregular verb *be*.

	SINGULAR	PLURAL
FIRST PERSON	I *am*	we *are*
SECOND PERSON	you *are*	you *are*
THIRD PERSON	he, she, it *is*	they *are*

Circle the correctly formed verb in each sentence.

1. Curling (is / am / are) a sport from 17th century Scotland.

2. Did you know that a curling match (is / am / are) played on ice?

3. There (is / am / are) four players on each team.

4. The team captain (is / am / are) the "skip."

5. Curling (is / am / are) very popular in Canada today.

6. (Is / Am / Are) you interested in seeing a curling match?

Don't let it confuse you when a group of words separates a subject and verb. Read the sentences below. Cross out the words that separate each subject and verb. Then circle the verb that agrees with the subject. The first one has been done for you.

1. The box ~~of chocolate candies~~ ((is) / are) for my aunt.

2. The book about dogs (tell / tells) how to build a dog house.

3. The bag of diamonds (is / are) the clue to the mystery.

4. Certain states, including Oregon, (welcome / welcomes) tourists.

5. The bowl of flowers (make / makes) a beautiful centerpiece.

6. The foreman, as well as the other workers, (is / are) leaving early.

USAGE NOTES

6. SUBJECT-VERB AGREEMENT DEMONS

The words *one*, *each*, *every*, *neither*, *either*, *everyone*, *nobody*, *everybody*, and *somebody* always take a singular verb.

EXAMPLE: *Neither* of these peaches *is* ripe enough to eat.

When *compound subjects* are joined by *and*, they are usually plural. Compound subjects joined by *or* are usually singular (unless the parts of the compound are plural themselves).

EXAMPLES: The *blue shirt **and** red tie **look*** good with those pants. (PLURAL)

A *sweater **or** light jacket **is*** warm enough on a spring day. (SINGULAR)

*Wool hat**s** **or** fleece headband**s** **keep*** ears very warm. (PLURAL)

Circle *is* or *are* to complete each sentence.

1. Everybody in the public schools (is / are) allowed to play sports.

2. Robert's coach and his father (is / are) proud of his progress.

3. Neither of my brothers (is / are) at home this evening.

4. None of the students' essays (is / are) completed.

Use the correct verb form to complete each sentence. The first one has been done for you.

1. **has / have**	Neither snails nor clams _____*has*_____ fur.
2. **belong / belongs**	Snails and clams _____ to an animal group called *mollusks*.
3. **has / have**	Each of these two creatures _____ a shell.
4. **is / are**	The octopus and the slug _____ mollusks that do not have shells.
5. **eat / eats**	Everybody I know _____ clams, squid, and snails.
6. **want / wants**	No one with any sense _____ to eat slugs.

Some words are plural in form, but singular in meaning. Treat these words as a singular subject.

EXAMPLES: Measles *is* a childhood disease.

Mathematics *is* my hardest class.

Words that tell how much and how many include *all*, *half*, *some*, *most*, and *none*. They are singular when used to tell how much. They are plural when used to tell how many.

EXAMPLES: Some of the milk *is* still in the glass. (How MUCH?)

Some of the students *are* absent today. (How MANY?)

Circle the correct verb form.

1. The Netherlands (is / are) famous for cheese and tulips.

2. Crazy Eights (is / are) my favorite card game.

3. Half the glass (is / are) still full of chocolate milk.

4. Half of the cars in the lot (cost / costs) too much.

5. All the boys in our class (is / are) wearing shorts today.

6. Did you notice that most of the butter (is / are) melted?

7. Gymnastics (requires / require) hours of practice each day.

8. Meals on Wheels (is / are) a service that takes food to shut-ins.

Use each of the following as the subject of a sentence: *the United States, mumps, checkers*. Make sure the subject and verb agree.

1. _____

2. _____

3. _____

Verbs change form to tell *when* something happens. Verb forms that show changes in time are called *tenses*. The ending *d* or *ed* is usually added to a verb to express *past tense*. The helping verbs *will* and *shall* are used to express *future tense*.

EXAMPLES: **PRESENT TENSE—HAPPENING NOW**
   I *deliver* pizza for Angelo's Pizzeria.

   PAST TENSE—HAPPENED IN THE PAST
   Last year I *delivered* for Pizza Pete's.

   FUTURE TENSE—WILL HAPPEN IN THE FUTURE
   Starting next week, I *will deliver* for Flying Pie Pizza.

A

Underline the verbs. Write *present, past,* or *future* to identify the tense.

1. _____ A helicopter is an amazing aircraft.

2. _____ It looks something like a wingless airplane.

3. _____ Propellers spin around on top.

4. _____ Some people call helicopters egg beaters.

5. _____ In World War II, helicopters proved their value.

6. _____ They moved the wounded from battlefields to hospitals.

7. _____ They rescued troops from behind enemy lines.

8. _____ Helicopters will save many lives in years to come.

9. _____ The industry will grow rapidly in the 21st century.

B

Imagine that you will soon take off on a magic carpet ride. Write three sentences describing what you will experience. Make sure the given verbs are in the future tense.

1. **(see)** _____

2. **(hear)** _____

3. **(feel)** _____

Not all verbs form the past tense by adding *d* or *ed*. *Irregular verbs* express the past tense with a change of spelling.

EXAMPLES: I usually *eat* lunch around noon. (PRESENT)

Yesterday I *ate* at 2:00 P.M. (PAST)

A

Underline an irregular *past tense* verb in each sentence. Then find the *present tense* form in the box and write it on the line. The first one has been done for you.

begin	steal	drive	ring	fall

1. Last night someone <u>stole</u> the bell from the bell tower. ____*steal*____

2. It rang at midnight but not at one o'clock. _____

3. Some thought that perhaps a thief drove off with it. _____

4. An odd silence fell over the town. _____

5. People began to think the bell was gone forever. _____

B

Write the verb form that correctly completes each sentence. The first one has been done for you.

1. The Incredible Shrinking Woman (shrink, shrank) ___*shrank*___ to the size of a fly.

2. Miller's Pond (freeze, froze) _____ solid last winter.

3. Do you (see, saw) _____ Margo very often?

4. We usually (eat, ate) _____ pizza on Tuesday nights.

5. Last Tuesday we (eat, ate) _____ fried rice and spring rolls instead.

6. The freak potato (grow, grew) _____ to the size of a watermelon.

32 — VERB PHRASES: ACTION IN THE PRESENT AND PAST

A verb phrase is made up of a main verb and one or more helping verbs. Use the ing ending to show continuing action in the present.

EXAMPLE:

HELPING VERB   MAIN VERB

The dancers **are taking** a lunch break.

VERB PHRASE

The helping verbs am, is, and are tell of action in the present. The helping verbs was and were show continuing action in the past.

EXAMPLES: Rosie **is telling** us a joke. (PRESENT)

Yesterday he **was attending** a conference. (PAST)

A

Underline the verb phrase in each sentence. Write HV above the *helping verb* and MV above the *main verb*.

1. Brad is hoping to buy his Uncle Abe's car.

2. He is saving a little money from each paycheck.

3. Last summer he was working at the supermarket.

4. Now he is delivering furniture on weekends.

5. Last month, Abe was asking $2,500 for his old Ford.

6. This month, however, he is asking only $2,000.

7. Brad's parents are willing to pay his car insurance.

B

Rewrite the verb in parentheses as a verb phrase. The first one has been done for you.

1. Sandra (wear) a new hat.   _is wearing_

2. You (go) on a long journey. _____

3. The workers (stay) later each day. _____

4. This plan (work) out really well. _____

5. Matt and Laura (get) married. _____

Action in the past is usually shown by adding *d, ed, n,* or *en* to the plural form of the main verb. The main verb usually follows a form of the helping verb *have.*

EXAMPLES: They ***are studying*** for the driver's test. (PRESENT)
    Many ***have taken*** the test before. (PAST)

Underline the verb phrase in each sentence. Then tell if it is in the *present* or *past* tense. The first one has been done for you.

1. Fifty students <u>are trying</u> out for the school play.   _*present*_

2. They are hoping for a part in *West Side Story*.   _____

3. My friend Anna has taken voice lessons.   _____

4. She is trying out for the role of Maria.   _____

5. Theresa has had no singing lessons at all.   _____

6. She has practiced on her own, however.   _____

7. Like Anna, Theresa is dreaming of the starring role.   _____

8. Everyone is waiting for the director's choice.   _____

D

Read the following paragraph. Underline the verb phrases. Then fill in the chart by writing the helping verbs and main verbs in order. The first one has been done for you.

The rain <u>has fallen</u> for 30 days. It has soaked the hillsides. Now the earth is starting to slide. Some homeowners are building concrete walls. Such walls have stopped landslides in the past. Everyone is praying that the walls hold and the sun shines.

HELPING VERB	PRESENT-TENSE MAIN VERB	PAST-TENSE MAIN VERB
has		*fallen*

A form of *do* is often used as a helping verb in a verb phrase, *Do* is used (1) to ask questions, (2) with the word *not*, and (3) for emphasis. When a main verb appears with *do*, it is always in plural form.

EXAMPLES:

Do you *wear* kneepads when you skateboard? (QUESTION)

I *did* not *wear* my kneepads last Saturday. (WITH *NOT*)

When I fell, I *did wish* I had them on! (EMPHASIS)

HAVE YOU NOTICED?

Sometimes another word will come between a helping verb and a main verb.

The dog *did* not *mind* the rain and mud. (WITH *NOT*)

I *did*, however, *notice* his dirty paws! (EMPHASIS)

Do you ever *allow* muddy pets in your house? (QUESTION)

A

Underline both the main verb and the helping verb in each verb phrase. Circle any words that come between the main verb and helping verb.

I did not expect guests. Did I invite you? I do sometimes forget these things. I am a bit surprised by your visit. Folks do not usually call on me at midnight.

B

Use verb phrases in three sentences. Be sure to include a form of the helping verb *do* along with the main verb.

1. **(to ask a question)** _____

_____

2. **(with the word *not*)** _____

_____

3. **(to add emphasis)** _____

_____

60

The helping verbs *will* and *shall* are used with a main verb to form the future tense.

EXAMPLES: All of that awful noise ***will stop*** soon.

Shall I ***pour*** you a glass of iced tea?

The helping verbs *can, could, may, might, must, should,* and *would* are also used in verb phrases.

EXAMPLES: The workers ***must finish*** the house by December.

The family ***can move*** in before the holidays.

 C

Underline *both* parts of the verb phrase in each sentence.

The painters will arrive tomorrow. They will probably paint the outside walls tan. We must see samples of the trim colors before choosing. We should select a color right away. We might choose navy blue. What color would you choose?

 D

Fill in the chart after you read the sentences. The first one has been done for you.

1. Someday you will probably hear about a volunteer group called Habitat for Humanity.

2. These volunteers will build more houses for needy families this year.

3. They might travel to all parts of the United States.

4. Some workers might not have any home-building experience.

5. They can be doctors, lawyers, teachers, or salespeople.

6. Jimmy Carter may be one of the most famous Habitat for Humanity volunteers.

	HELPING VERB	MAIN VERB
1.	*will*	*hear*
2.		
3.		
4.		
5.		
6.		

7. PASSIVE VERB PHRASES

Most sentences are written in the *active voice*. This means that the subject performs the action. In sentences written in the *passive voice*, the subject receives the action. To write in the passive voice, use a form of the helping verb *be* and a past tense verb.

EXAMPLES: Mike *gave* us tickets to the circus. (active voice)

We *were given* circus tickets. (passive voice)

Remember that *most* of what you read is in the active voice. Writers usually use the passive voice when they don't know who or what performed the action.

EXAMPLE: The note *was written* in unfamiliar handwriting.

A

Write *AV* before sentences written in the *active voice*. Write *PV* before sentences written in the *passive voice*.

1. _____ P. T. Barnum owned the Barnum and Bailey Circus.

2. _____ He once said, "There's a sucker born every minute."

3. _____ Unusual circus acts were always needed.

4. _____ Barnum once offered $10,000 to anyone who could fool him.

5. _____ Soon he was contacted by a man with a cherry-colored cat.

6. _____ Barnum offered to put the cat in a circus act.

7. _____ The cat was sent to him in a shipping box.

8. _____ Barnum found an ordinary black cat and a short note inside the box.

9. _____ The note said, "Maine cherries are black. There is a sucker born every minute!"

B

Look back at the sentences in Part A that are written in the passive voice. Rewrite them in the *active voice*.

1. _____

2. _____

3. _____

8. SHIFTS IN VERB TENSE

Good writers usually avoid shifting verb tense within a sentence, paragraph, or essay. They decide at the start whether they will use present, past, or future tense. Then they stick to that choice.

At times, however, there is a good reason to change verb tense in a sentence. Sometimes the actions actually happen at different times.

EXAMPLES: I *am sure* that I *will win* first place.

                  PRESENT   FUTURE

A ──────────────────────────────

Study the verb tense in each sentence. Write *present, past,* or *future.*

1. On April 1, many people celebrate April Fool's Day. _____

2. Britons first celebrated this day in the 1600s. _____

3. On this day, friends play pranks on each other. _____

4. Last year, my friend played a trick on me. _____

5. This year, I am planning to get back at him! _____

B ──────────────────────────────

Read the paragraph. Underline the *present tense* verbs and circle the *past tense* verbs.

    It was April Fool's Day. Carrie planned to trick her friend Rich. She puts a gift-wrapped box in his locker. Rich found the box and is excited. He does not see the air holes in the back. Rich took the box out of his locker and quickly opens it. Out jumps a big green toad!

C ──────────────────────────────

Rewrite the paragraph above so that *all* verbs are either past or present tense.

_____

_____

_____

_____

_____

9. TROUBLESOME VERBS: *lie* and *lay*, *sit* and *set*,

Certain pairs of verbs are often confused. Why? Because the meanings of the words are very similar and both words sound alike.

lie   MEANING: to be or remain in a horizontal position; to rest
    VERB FORMS: *lie, lay, (has) lain, (is) lying*
    EXAMPLE: I often *lie* on the couch to watch TV.

lay   MEANING: to put something down or to place it somewhere
    VERB FORMS: *lay, laid, (has) laid, (is) laying*
    EXAMPLE: I *laid* my glasses somewhere in this room.
    (Hint: Lay—meaning *put*—always takes an object. In the example above, the object is *glasses*.)

sit   MEANING: to rest or to occupy a seat
    VERB FORMS: *sit, sat, (has) sat, (is) sitting*
    EXAMPLE: The cat *sat* happily in the sun.

set   MEANING: to put or to place in position
    VERB FORMS: *set, set, (has) set, (is) setting*
    EXAMPLE: She carefully *sets* the chess pieces on the board.

A

Circle the correct verbs.

1. The sun (sat / set) in the west.

2. Don't just (sit / set) there!

3. (Sit / Set) those flowers down.

4. Please (sit / set) the table.

5. We will (lie / lay) the tiles first.

6. (Lie / lay) in the hammock.

B

Cross out each incorrect verb. Write the correction above it. The first error has been corrected as an example.

Thanksgiving is a time when my family and friends ~~set~~ *sit* down together for dinner. Someone cooks a fine meal and sits out their best dishes. I live in Hawaii, and we often set outside for dinner. My Aunt Hannah likes to lie an orchid on each plate. After dinner, I sit all the plates on a tray and take them to the kitchen to wash. Some lucky guests just lay around relaxing!

bring and *take*, *leave* and *let*, *borrow* and *lend*

USAGE NOTES

bring   MEANING: to carry something to the one speaking
           EXAMPLE: Vinny will **bring** his homework to my house.

take   MEANING: to carry or move something away from the one speaking
           EXAMPLE: Did you **take** the video back to the store?
           (Hint: *Bring* is related to *come*; *take* is related to *go*.)

leave   MEANING: to let stay or be; to depart
           EXAMPLE: You can **leave** your book on the table.

let   MEANING: to allow or permit something
           EXAMPLE: Mrs. Jenkins **let** Junior jump on the bed.

borrow MEANING: to take something to use for a while
           EXAMPLE: I **borrowed** my cousin's skis last weekend.

lend   MEANING: to let someone use something for a while
           EXAMPLE: Our neighbors **lend** us their lawn mower.

C

Circle the correct verbs in each sentence. Then write *two* original sentences using each of the verbs you circled. The first one has been *half* done for you.

1. (Bring / (Take)) me out to the ball game. (Bring / Take) me some snacks.
   I will take an umbrella to the game in case it rains.
   _____

2. If we (let / leave) that early, will you (let / leave) me drive?
   _____
   _____

3. If you (lend / borrow) me your catcher's mitt, I'll let you (lend / borrow) my dirt bike.
   _____
   _____

A   Underline each verb. Write **AV** for **action verb** and **LV** for **linking verb**.

1. _____ In the early 1940s, no African-Americans pitched in the major leagues.

2. _____ Satchel Paige was a great pitcher, however.

3. _____ The famous pitcher Dizzy Dean knew it.

4. _____ In 1948, the Cleveland Indians put Paige on their pitching mound.

5. _____ At age 42, Paige had finally reached the big leagues.

6. _____ He was baseball's oldest rookie.

B   Circle the verb form that correctly completes each sentence. Then write that verb on the line.

1. Our sense of smell (is / are) important. _____

2. It (protect / protects) us from many dangers. _____

3. A bad smell (warn / warns) us that food is spoiled. _____

4. (Smell / Smells) something around you right now. _____

5. What can you (learns / learn) from the way it smells? _____

6. Another of your senses (act / acts) as a warning device. _____

7. Each nerve ending in your fingers (stop / stops) you from burning yourself. _____

8. These nerve endings (send / sends) messages to the brain. _____

9. (Think / Thinks) about things you can feel right now. _____

10. (Is / Are) your shoes too tight? _____

11. Do the threads of your sweater (feel / feels) itchy? _____

C Underline each verb. Tell if the verb form is *past, present,* or *future* tense. Then tell if it agrees with a *singular* or *plural* subject. The first one has been done for you.

1. Charlie Chaplin <u>was</u> a British-born comedian.   *past, singular*

2. He came to America in 1913.   _____

3. Moviegoers loved him.   _____

4. His films still play in theaters.   _____

5. Everyone knows his name.   _____

6. My friend and I will go to a Charlie Chaplin film festival next week.   _____

7. Either he or I will buy the tickets.   _____

D Write the correct form of the verb in parentheses.

1. One of Chaplin's characters (make) _____ him a star.

2. That character (be) _____ "the little tramp."

3. In 1915, people first (see) _____ the little tramp in a movie.

4. That Chaplin film (become) _____ a huge hit.

5. In 1917, Chaplin (earn) _____ an amazing $1 million.

E Underline each verb phrase. Write **HV** above each **helping verb** and **MV** above each **main verb**.

1. Vic has practiced the long jump daily for five years.

2. He is hoping to be like Olympic champ Carl Lewis.

3. Lewis has won long jump gold medals four years in a row.

4. London, England, is hosting the 2012 Olympic Games.

ADJECTIVES AND ADVERBS

34 — RECOGNIZING ADJECTIVES

An *adjective* is a word that describes a noun or pronoun. Adjectives add further meaning or detail to the nouns they describe. An adjective most often comes *before* a noun or *after* a linking verb.

EXAMPLES: Sour flavors pucker lips.
ADJECTIVE   NOUN

Lemons are sour.
NOUN   LINKING VERB   ADJECTIVE

A

See how an adjective adds to the meaning of a noun. Underline each adjective. Draw a picture of the noun it describes.

1. a messy desk

2. a tidy desk

3. a broken desk

B

Underline the adjectives. The first sentence has been done for you.

1. The <u>tiny</u> lighthouse stood on the <u>rocky</u> island.

2. The bright light warned weary sailors of danger.

3. One dark night, a fierce storm arose offshore.

4. The foamy waves were high, and the wind was wild.

5. A lonely young man lived in the lighthouse.

6. He made sure to turn on the brilliant light.

7. Some lost sailors saw the light through the dense gray fog.

8. They steered away from the dangerous rocks and shallow bay.

9. Thanks to the sturdy little lighthouse, they were safe.

C

Underline the adjectives in the paragraph. Then circle the noun or pronoun each adjective describes.

Biloxi, Mississippi, is a delightful resort town. It is beautiful and charming. Biloxi sits beside the warm waters of the Gulf of Mexico. Neighborhoods of old stucco cottages remind visitors of an earlier era. Huge mossy oaks line the brick streets there.

D

Rewrite each sentence. Add one or more adjectives to describe each noun. The first sentence has been done for you.

1. The town held a celebration.

   The quaint seaside town held a noisy fireworks celebration.

2. The boy entered the room.

   _____

3. A flower bloomed in the garden.

   _____

4. The woman slammed the door.

   _____

5. A cat lay in the yard.

   _____

E

Choose two sentences from Part D. Rewrite each one, using different adjectives to create completely different pictures.

_____

_____

⬡35 ＝ ARTICLES

The words *a, an,* and *the* are special adjectives called *articles*. They come before nouns in sentences. Use *the* when talking about a particular person or thing. Use *a* and *an* when talking about a general group.

EXAMPLES: I want to see **the** movie. (SPECIFIC MOVIE)
I want to see **a** movie. (ANY MOVIE)

Use *a* before a word that begins with a consonant. Use *an* before a word that begins with a vowel.

EXAMPLES: That creature in the bush is **a** rabbit.
That creature in the rafters is **an** owl.

Use *a* and *an* only with singular nouns. Use *the* with singular or plural nouns.

EXAMPLES: I found **a** penny.
I found **the** penny that you lost.
I found **the** pennies that you lost.

⬡A⟩─────────────────────────────────

Read the paragraph. Then circle all the *articles*.

During the Civil War, the North and the South fought a battle in Tupelo, Mississippi. For years Tupelo was a busy railroad town. Later it became the hometown of the "King of Rock 'n' Roll." The King was born in a small white house. When he grew up he became a singer and an actor. Do you know the name of the famous man from Tupelo? Tupelo was the birthplace of the great Elvis Presley.

⬡B⟩─────────────────────────────────

Write *a, an,* or *the* on the lines.

1. *Life with Bertha* is _____ amusing TV show.

2. It is about _____ very funny lady and _____ people in her office.

3. One time, Bertha decided to leave _____ office early.

4. She put _____ big, long pillow in her desk chair.

5. She dressed the pillow in _____ hat and _____ overcoat.

6. From _____ back, _____ pillow looked just like Bertha.

70

Most adjectives can appear either before or after nouns. The adjectives in the box, however, can only be used *before* nouns.

a	an	another	any	both
each	either	every	few	many
most	neither	one	several	some
that	the	these	this	those

HAVE YOU NOTICED?

The articles *a, an,* and *the* are "before-the-noun-only" adjectives.

A

Read the paragraph. Circle adjectives shown in the box above.

Many people think of the Wright brothers as the inventors of the airplane. In 1902, these brothers did successfully fly. But several inventors had been dreaming of flight much earlier. In 1842, an English inventor, William Samuel Hensen, designed a plane powered by steam. About 50 years later, in 1893, Sir Hiram Maxim built this type of plane. The engine had 300 horsepower. That plane crashed in 1894. Sir Hiram was trying to fly in a circle above a track.

B

Use adjectives from the box to complete the sentences. (There may be more than one correct choice.) Then circle the noun each adjective describes. The first one has been done for you.

1. ___*Several*___ (suitcases) were lost when we changed planes.

2. _____ airline promised that _____ bags would be found.

3. _____ suitcases were not only found but delivered to us.

4. _____ piece of luggage was in perfect condition.

5. _____ same thing happened to me on _____ trip.

6. Now I put _____ tag on _____ bag I take on _____ plane.

35 ADJECTIVES AFTER LINKING VERBS

Adjectives often appear after linking verbs. These adjectives are called *predicate adjectives*. They tell about the noun or pronoun that serves as the subject of the sentence.

EXAMPLES: The restaurant was crowded.

NOUN   LINKING VERB   PREDICATE ADJECTIVE

It was hot and noisy.

PRONOUN   LINKING VERB   PREDICATE ADJECTIVES

A

Underline each predicate adjective. Draw an arrow to the noun or pronoun it describes.

1. The weather is wet and cold.

2. The sky looks dark.

3. The clouds are thick.

4. The fire in the fireplace is bright and cheery.

5. It seems inviting.

6. Some hot tea and toast would be delicious.

B

Complete each sentence by adding predicate adjectives. The first one has been done for you.

1. The coat was ___*thick*___ and ___*warm*___ .

2. My friend is _____ and _____ .

3. A book should be _____ and _____ .

C

Write two sentences containing predicate adjectives. Use one adjective that describes color and one that describes size.

1. _____

2. _____

Sometimes you will use the adjective form of a proper noun. Like proper nouns, *proper adjectives* refer to the names of particular persons, places, things, events, and ideas.

EXAMPLES: The party had a **Hawaiian** theme.

My **English** class is reading *Hamlet*.

HAVE YOU NOTICED?

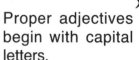

Proper adjectives begin with capital letters.

A

Draw a line to match each proper adjective on the left with the noun it would most likely describe.

1.	Hawaiian	a. turkey
2.	Thanksgiving	b. luau
3.	United States	c. comedy
4.	Shakespearean	d. automobile
5.	Chevrolet	e. government

B

Write a sentence using a proper adjective/noun pair from Part A.

_____

_____

C

Circle the proper adjectives. Then underline the nouns they describe.

We drove to Vancouver, British Columbia. After a stop at the Canadian border, we continued north to the city. There we admired the Vancouver skyline of tall buildings and white-capped mountains. We sampled fish from Canadian waters and found terrific Indian, Thai, Italian, and Chinese restaurants. Our Vancouver mornings began with strolls along the Stanley Park walkway. We ended each day watching the sunset at English Bay.

⬡39 — POSSESSIVE NOUNS AND PRONOUNS USED AS ADJECTIVES

Possessive nouns and *possessive pronouns* act as adjectives when they describe the nouns they precede.

EXAMPLES: I read the ***students'*** essays. (possessive noun used as adjective)
Their ideas were interesting. (possessive pronoun used as adjective)

⬡A

Underline the possessive nouns and pronouns that are used as adjectives. Draw arrows to the nouns they describe. The first one has been done for you.

1. A cat's senses are really quite remarkable.

2. The cat uses its paws to check out its surroundings.

3. Its hearing is sharper than a human's hearing.

4. A cat's eyesight, however, is not very good in the daytime.

5. Most cats can see their prey much better in dim light.

6. Have you ever seen your cat's eyes glow at night?

7. The cat's inner eye is a layer of pink, gold, blue, and green cells.

8. The cells reflect light, which helps the animal's night vision.

⬡B

Write five original sentences. Use the listed possessive nouns and pronouns as adjectives.

1. **girls'** _____

2. **his** _____

3. **mouse's** _____

4. **student's** _____

5. **my** _____

You can use adjectives to compare two or more people, places, or things.

The *comparative form* compares two things. For example: My puppy is *smaller* than hers. The *superlative* form compares more than two things. For example: Of all the puppies in the dog show, mine was the *smallest*.

Most one-syllable adjectives and some two-syllable adjectives form the comparative by adding the suffix *er*. The superlative is formed by adding *est*.

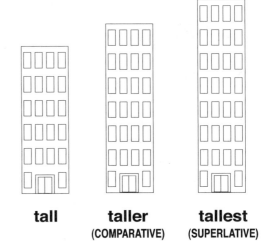

tall **taller** **tallest**
(COMPARATIVE) (SUPERLATIVE)

 A

Complete the chart with the missing forms of each adjective.

	COMPARATIVE	SUPERLATIVE
1. weak	weaker	
2. plain		plainest
3.	happier	happiest
4. dark	darker	
5. clean		

B

Choose one of the adjectives from Part A. Write a sentence using each form.

1. **(comparative)** _____

2. **(superlative)** _____

40

To form the comparative and superlative forms of some two-syllable adjectives, use *more* or *most* before the adjective. *More* or *most* are also used before all adjectives with three or more syllables.

EXAMPLES:

POSITIVE	COMPARATIVE	SUPERLATIVE
hopeful	more hopeful	most hopeful
exciting	more exciting	most exciting

C

Write *C* or *S* to tell if the boldfaced adjective form is *comparative* or *superlative*.

1. _____ Hawaii is one of the **most popular** vacation spots.

2. _____ People expect the island weather to be **more balmy** than the mainland climate.

3. _____ Hawaii also has some of the world's **most spectacular** scenery.

4. _____ Hawaii's Mt. Waialeale is the **wettest** spot in the world.

D

Decide if each statement requires the *comparative* or *superlative* form of the adjective given. Write the correct form on the line.

1. Emmitt Smith was one of the (great) _____ touchdown scorers of all time.

2. In 1994, he was chosen the (valuable) _____ player in Super Bowl XXVIII.

3. In recent years, the Honda Accord has been the automobile industry's (big) _____ seller.

4. The Accord has been (popular) _____ than the Nissan Altima.

76

IRREGULAR ADJECTIVE FORMS — ⬡41

Some adjectives are irregular. The comparative and superlative forms are not made in the usual way. Study the irregular adjectives listed in the chart.

POSITIVE	COMPARATIVE	SUPERLATIVE
good	better	best
bad	worse	worst
many/much	more	most

⬡**A**

Circle the correct adjective. Identify the form as *comparative* or *superlative*.

1. One of the (good / best) known dogs is a collie called Lassie.

   _____

2. (More / Most) people have read *Lassie Come Home* than have read *Lad: A Dog*.

   _____

3. No dog could be (good / better) than Buck from Jack London's *Call of the Wild*.

   _____

4. It's hard to say whether Lassie or Buck faced (worse / worst) problems.

   _____

⬡**B**

Decide whether or not each boldfaced adjective form is correct. If it is correct, write *C* above the adjective. If it is incorrect, cross it out and write the correct adjective form above it.

1. Hurricane Katrina was among the **worse** storms in recent times.

2. Today weather forecasters have **good** tools than in the past.

3. Scientists are **best** able to predict hurricanes than earthquakes.

4. The Indian Ocean quake of 2004 was the **worse** quake in years.

USING LESS AND LEAST TO COMPARE

Sometimes comparisons are made by using *less* and *least* rather than *more* and *most*. Use *less* when comparing two people or things. Use *least* when comparing three or more people or things.

EXAMPLES: My second airplane trip was **less** exciting than my first.
Which is the **least** interesting of your classes this year?

A

Complete the sentences by adding *less* or *least*.

1. What is the _____ amount you can pay for a good used car?

2. A used Chevy is _____ expensive than a used Saab.

3. Vanilla is my _____ favorite ice cream flavor.

4. A bowl of strawberries is _____ fattening than a piece of pie.

5. Today's weather is _____ breezy than yesterday's.

B

Use *more, most, less,* or *least* in five original sentences that compare:

1. **(two of your classes)** _____

_____

2. **(some of your hobbies)** _____

_____

3. **(two holidays)** _____

_____

4. **(places you have lived)** _____

_____

5. **(people in your family)** _____

_____

10. SPELLING COMPARATIVE ADJECTIVES

A change of spelling occurs when you write the comparative forms of some adjectives. Remember these rules:

- Some one-syllable adjectives—like *fat*—end with a consonant preceded by a vowel. Before adding *er* or *est* to these adjectives, you will double the final consonant.

    EXAMPLES: **fat, fatter, fattest**   **hot, hotter, hottest**

- Some adjectives—like *happy*—end with a *y* preceded by a consonant. Change the *y* to *i* before adding *er* or *est* to these adjectives.

    EXAMPLES: **happy, happier, happiest**   **lucky, luckier, luckiest**

 A

Complete the chart by filling in the missing forms of each adjective.

		COMPARATIVE	SUPERLATIVE
1.	dusty	dustier	
2.	wet		wettest
3.	snowy		
4.	angry		

B

Write the correctly spelled adjective form on the line.

1. I feel (lucky) _____ today than I have in years.

2. This could be the (big) _____ day of my life!

3. It may sound like the (crazy) _____ idea in the world, but I'm going to look for money in the sand.

4. The sand at this time of day is (hot) _____ than a stove top.

5. Ow! This could be the (silly) _____ thing I've ever done.

6. It may be (easy) _____ to work for my money than to search through the hot sand.

11. USING SPECIFIC ADJECTIVES

You can make your written ideas clearer by using *specific* rather than *general* adjectives. Notice the adjectives *nice* and *generous* in the example sentences. Decide which adjective gives you a more exact idea about what the next door neighbor does.

EXAMPLES: My next door neighbor is **nice**.

My next door neighbor is **generous**.

Nice is a very general word. There are many things a person can do to be considered *nice*. The adjective *generous* is much more specific. A *generous* person unselfishly gives to others.

A

Circle the more *specific* adjective in each pair. *Hint:* Ask yourself which adjective creates a clearer picture.

1. bad / naughty

2. old / decayed

3. scorching / hot

4. booming / loud

5. wet / drenched

6. dirty / polluted

7. ear-splitting / loud

8. muffled / quiet

9. crimson / red

10. tall / towering

B

Next to each general adjective, write a more specific one.

1. clean _____

2. smart _____

3. good _____

4. big _____

5. blue _____

6. young _____

C

Describe each noun with a specific adjective.

1. snow _____

2. the moon _____

3. a rose _____

4. tomato soup_____

An *adverb* usually describes a verb. It adds further meaning or detail to the verb by telling how, when, where, or how often.

EXAMPLES: The injured boy walked ***slowly***. (*How* did the boy walk?)

He fell ***yesterday***. (*When* did the accident happen?)

The accident occurred ***upstairs***. (*Where* did the accident happen?)

Active children ***frequently*** fall down. (*How often* do they fall?)

 A

Underline the adverb in each sentence. Then write it on the chart under the question it answers. The first one has been done for you.

1. The flamingo struts <u>gracefully</u> on its long legs.

2. Its deep red feathers glow nightly in the moonlight.

3. The big bird often stands on one leg.

4. These birds eat oddly.

5. They dunk their heads underwater.

6. They sift quickly through the mud.

7. They usually find small shellfish.

8. Flamingos are shy and never attack humans.

9. The ancient Romans sometimes served flamingo tongues at their feasts.

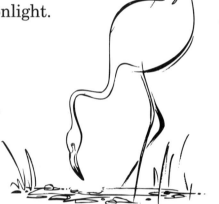

HOW?	WHEN?	HOW OFTEN?	WHERE?
1. *gracefully*			
2.			
3.			
4.			
5.			
6.			
7.			
8.			
9.			

Adverbs are also used to tell more about adjectives or other adverbs. They add meaning by telling *how much*, *how little*, *how often*, and *to what degree*.

EXAMPLES: The swarming wasps seemed very angry,
ADV.   ADJ.

The beekeeper had rather stupidly disturbed their nest.
ADV.   ADV.

B

Circle each adverb. Draw an arrow to the word it describes. The first one has been done for you.

1. The fire fighters unreeled the hoses (very)(quickly.)

2. They approached the burning building rather cautiously.

3. The flames were extremely hot.

4. The rescue workers had to be especially careful.

5. They did not want to be trapped inside the smoky building.

Underline each adverb. The first one has been done for you.

In Colonial times, people <u>generously</u> volunteered to fight fires. The strongest volunteers passed very heavy buckets from a well to the fire. Then women and children quickly passed the emptied buckets back to the well. These extremely hard-working townspeople were appropriately called the *bucket brigade*.

First list the adverbs from Part C in the chart below. Next tell what word each adverb describes. Then identify that word as a *verb*, *adjective,* or *adverb*. The first one has been done for you.

ADVERB	WORD DESCRIBED		ADVERB	WORD DESCRIBED
1. *generously*	*volunteered (verb)*	4.		
2.		5.		
3.		6.		

Remember that adverbs are used to add detail to verbs, adjectives, or other adverbs.

A

Complete the answer to each question with an adverb from the box. More than one choice may be correct.

yesterday	carefully	upstairs	later	often	very
regularly	slightly	seldom	hard	uncomfortably	

1. **When will you do your homework?**

   I will do it _____.

2. **When did the painters finish the house?**

   They finished the job _____

3. **How did the painters do their work?**

   They did it _____.

4. **Where is the main bedroom?**

   The main bedroom is _____.

5. **How hot is the room?**

   The room is _____ hot.

6. **How often are Scott and Randy absent?**

   Scott and Randy are _____ absent.

7. **How hard is it raining?**

   It is raining _____.

B

Choose three adverbs from the box. Use each one in an original sentence.

1. _____

2. _____

3. _____

Adverbs that describe verbs can often be placed in different parts of a sentence without changing its meaning.

EXAMPLES: ***Suddenly***, it started raining.
It ***suddenly*** started raining.
It started raining ***suddenly***.

Adverbs that describe adjectives and adverbs usually come *before* the word they describe.

EXAMPLES: Your gift makes me ***very*** happy.
The elevator rose ***extremely*** rapidly.

Underline the adverb in each sentence. Then rewrite the sentence, changing the adverb's position. The first one has been done for you.

1. The audience applauded <u>wildly</u>.

   The audience wildly applauded.

2. The school play was clearly a success.

   _____

3. The costumes were designed brilliantly.

   _____

4. We sometimes eat at the Hilltop Cafe.

   _____

5. Usually, the food is delicious and inexpensive.

   _____

6. Would you like to join me for lunch tomorrow?

   _____

You can use adverbs to compare two or more actions. Adverb forms are similar to forms of adjectives. Add the suffix *er* to very short adverbs to compare two actions (comparative form). Add *est* to these short adverbs to compare more than two (superlative form). Add *more* or *less* or *most* or *least* before longer adverbs. The adverb *well* is irregular.

	COMPARATIVE	SUPERLATIVE
early	earlier	earliest
slowly	more slowly	most slowly
well	better	best

EXAMPLES: I hope the mail carrier arrives **early** today.

Yesterday, she came **earlier** than usual. (COMPARATIVE)

The **earliest** she has ever arrived is about 9 o'clock. (SUPERLATIVE)

A

Circle the correct form of the adverb. On the line write *C* if the adverb is *comparative*, *S* if it is *superlative*, or *N* if it is a *noncomparative* adverb. The first one has been done for you.

1. __S__ The cheetah is the (fast / faster /(fastest)) of all land animals.

2. _____ The tiger moves (swiftly / less swiftly / least swiftly) than the cheetah.

3. _____ It is (well / better / best) suited than the lion for chasing its prey.

4. _____ I named my cat Cheetah because she is the (fast / faster / fastest) cat I know.

5. _____ She hunts (well / better / best) than my last cat, Slowpoke.

6. _____ When Cheetah gets into a fight, she howls (fiercely / more fiercely / most fiercely) than her opponent.

B

Using the adverb *loudly*, write one original sentence for each form.

1. **(comparative)** _____

2. **(superlative)** _____

12. AVOIDING DOUBLE NEGATIVES

Never and *not* are *negative adverbs*. When these words are used with a verb, the action is canceled or the state of being is denied.

EXAMPLES: Walter **never** eats breakfast.   I am **not** ready for the test.

Avoid double negatives. Use only one negative word in a sentence. Negative words include *no, not, never, no one, nobody, nothing, nowhere, none, hardly, barely,* and *scarcely*.

EXAMPLES: I **didn't** do **nothing** wrong. (Incorrect—double negative)

I did **nothing** wrong. (Correct—one negative)

I did **not** do anything wrong. (Correct—one negative)

A

Write *C* in the blank if the sentence is correct.
Put a check mark (✓) if you see a double negative.

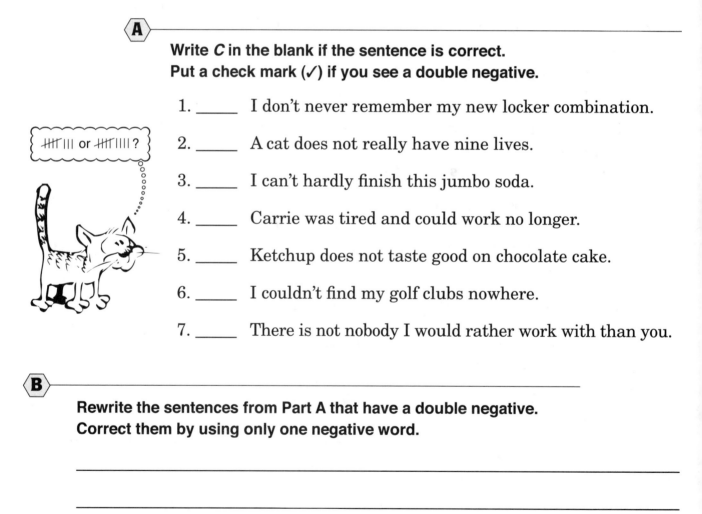

1. _____ I don't never remember my new locker combination.

2. _____ A cat does not really have nine lives.

3. _____ I can't hardly finish this jumbo soda.

4. _____ Carrie was tired and could work no longer.

5. _____ Ketchup does not taste good on chocolate cake.

6. _____ I couldn't find my golf clubs nowhere.

7. _____ There is not nobody I would rather work with than you.

B

Rewrite the sentences from Part A that have a double negative.
Correct them by using only one negative word.

_____

_____

_____

_____

13. ADJECTIVE OR ADVERB?

USAGE NOTES

Choose *adjectives* or *adverbs* carefully. Remember that adjectives can only describe nouns and pronouns. Adverbs describe only verbs, adjectives, and other adverbs.

EXAMPLES: **INCORRECT**   **CORRECT**

I finished the test **quick**.   I finished the test **quickly**.

The describing words *good* and *well* can be troublemakers. People sometimes use *good*, which is an adjective, when the adverb *well* is called for. Always use *well* to describe an *action*.

EXAMPLES: **INCORRECT**   **CORRECT**

I play tennis **good**.   I play tennis **well**.

 A

Circle the correct describing word. Draw an arrow to the word it describes. The first one has been done for you.

1. In school, Lynn dressed (odd /(oddly)) but (attractive /(attractively)).

2. She wore an (unusual / unusually) dress to the class party.

3. The hem of her dress was (uneven / unevenly).

4. Some people stared at Lynn (curious / curiously).

5. Others were (rude / rudely) and laughed (loud / loudly).

6. "Take a (good / well) look!" Lynn told them.

7. The next day at school, at least 20 students had hemmed their skirts and pants (uneven / unevenly).

8. Lynn is now doing (real / really) (good / well) as a dress designer.

B

Write sentences using these adjectives and adverbs: *good, well, bad, badly*.

1. _____

2. _____

3. _____

4. _____

A To find the mystery word (reads down), use the clues to complete the puzzle.

1. a word used to describe a noun or pronoun

2. two words combined in a shortened form

3. the special adjectives *a, an,* and *the*

4. word that describes a verb, an adjective, or an adverb

5. a word that indicates "no"

1. __ __ __ | d | __ __ __ __ __ __

2. __ __ __ __ __ | s | __ __ __ __

3. __ __ __ | r | __ __ __ __

4. __ __ __ __ __ | |

5. __ | | __ __ __ __ __ __

B Write **T** or **F** to tell whether each statement is *true* or *false*.

1. _____ Adjectives can only be used before nouns.

2. _____ A predicate adjective comes before a linking verb.

3. _____ Adjectives and adverbs have two forms of comparison, *neutral* and *negative*.

4. _____ The comparative form is used to make a comparison between two things or actions.

5. _____ The superlative form is used to compare more than two things or actions.

6. _____ The suffix *er* or the words *more* or *less* are often used to form the comparative.

7. _____ The suffix *est* or the words *most* or *least* are often used to form the superlative.

8. _____ Good writers often use double negatives.

9. _____ The word *good* is an irregular adverb.

10. _____ The word *well* is an irregular adverb.

C Underline the *adjectives*. Circle the *adverbs*.

1. Events often affect fashions.

2. World War II brought big changes in U.S. styles.

3. American designers quickly adjusted to the shortage of cloth.

4. They cleverly created women's blouses with shorter sleeves.

5. Short skirts soon replaced longer ones.

6. Many women seldom wore skirts.

7. Slacks were more practical for wartime factory jobs.

D Circle the *adjectives* or *adverbs* that correctly complete the sentences.

1. In 1900, a (good / well) dressed gentleman wore a vest, jacket, and (soft / softly) hat.

2. A (proper / properly) dressed lady never showed her (bare / barely) ankles.

3. Children's clothes were (real / really) (uncomfortable / uncomfortably).

4. Both boys and girls wore (heavy / heavily) underwear.

E Write the *adjective* or *adverb* form needed to make a comparison.

1. In the 1920s, young men wore trousers with the (wide) _____ legs they could find.

2. Pants called Oxford Bags were (big) _____ around at the legs than they were around the waist.

3. The (classy) _____ jacket of the decade was a raccoon coat.

PREPOSITIONS

FOR HELP WITH THIS UNIT, SEE THE REFERENCE GUIDE, RULES 37–43.

UNIT
6

(47) RECOGNIZING PREPOSITIONS AND PREPOSITIONAL PHRASES

A *preposition* shows the relationship between a noun and other words in a sentence. A preposition is always part of a word group called a *prepositional phrase*. The phrase may come at the beginning, middle, or end of a sentence. It begins with the preposition and ends with a noun or pronoun. That noun or pronoun is the *object* of the *preposition*.

EXAMPLES:

PREPOSITIONAL PHRASE

He hid the coin *under his hat.*

PREPOSITION OBJECT

PREPOSITIONAL PHRASE

We hurried *through the crowd.*

PREPOSITION OBJECT

A

Study each boldfaced prepositional phrase. Circle the preposition that begins it. Then draw a line under the object of the preposition. The first one has been done for you.

1. The detective stood (under) the **streetlight**.

2. The building **across the street** seemed deserted.

3. The detective thought a thief was **in it**.

4. **For many hours** he waited patiently.

5. He buttoned his overcoat **against the cold wind**.

B

Underline all prepositional phrases. Then circle each preposition and draw a second line under each preposition's object.

At last, the door of the building swung open with a loud bang. A dark figure moved down the steps toward the bus stop. No one was on the street with the two men except a black cat. The light by the bus stop lit the dark figure's face. "Oops! Wrong man," thought the detective.

Nearly all prepositions are short words.

C

Use a preposition from the box to complete each sentence. There may be more than one correct choice, and you may use a preposition more than once.

within	under	to	through	into	in	over	throughout

1. There is very hot, melted rock deep _____ the earth.

2. Sometimes this rock rises _____ the surface.

3. It flows _____ cracks and openings called vents.

4. Lava piles grow _____ mountains we call volcanoes.

5. Some volcanoes rise _____ just a few years.

6. Other volcanoes form slowly _____ the centuries.

D

Choose a preposition from the box to match each meaning. Then use the clues to solve the puzzle. The first one has been done for you.

above	before	behind	beside	between	during	except	like	near	with

ACROSS

1. happening at an earlier time
2. overhead
5. aside from, excluding
7. happening at the same time
9. next to

DOWN

1. in the rear of
3. in the middle of
4. close at hand
6. similar to
8. in the company of

(Crossword grid: 1 ACROSS answer filled in as B E F O R E)

48 — THE OBJECT OF THE PREPOSITION

The *object of the preposition* is always a *noun* or a *pronoun*. Often the object directly follows the preposition. Sometimes other words come between the preposition and the object.

PREP. OBJECT

EXAMPLES: It is courteous to be quiet *in libraries*.

PREP.   OBJECT

In the nonfiction *section*, books are arranged by call numbers.

When the object of the preposition is a pronoun, the prepositional phrase usually has only two words.

EXAMPLE: The library will reserve books *for me*.

A

Underline the prepositions. Then circle their objects.

HOME SWEET HOME

1. Every night Steve plays CDs in his room.

2. His favorites are songs from the past.

3. He often sings along with the tunes.

4. He listens to the Beatles and sings, "We all live in a yellow submarine!"

5. "Does your chewing gum lose its flavor on the bedpost overnight?" asks another song.

B

Complete each sentence by adding a prepositional phrase. Then underline your preposition and circle the object of the preposition.

1. The thunder _____.

2. The animals _____ were frightened.

3. The wind blew _____.

4. A big storm was _____.

Some words can be adverbs **or** prepositions. The part of speech depends on how they are used in a sentence. Remember that a preposition must be part of a phrase, and it must have an object. An adverb does *not* have an object.

EXAMPLES: Clouds drifted *above*.
ADVERB

Clouds drifted *above* our *heads*.
PREP.   OBJECT

A

Write A or P to tell whether each boldfaced word is an *adverb* or a *preposition*.

1. _____ Everyplace I go is filled **with** warnings.

2. _____ A park sign says, "Don't walk **on** the grass."

3. _____ The street sign **outside** my school warns drivers.

4. _____ It tells them to slow **down**.

5. _____ Every time I go **outside**, I am greeted by a sign.

6. _____ There is no parking **on** this street.

7. _____ There is no diving **off** this pier.

8. _____ Warnings greet me as I walk or drive **about**.

9. _____ I look **up**, and the red light means stop.

10. _____ I look **down**, and a double line tells me not to pass.

11. _____ I can't step **off** the curb when the light says WAIT.

12. _____ Sometimes I get tired **of** so many warnings.

13. _____ Living **without** them would be dangerous, however!

B

Write two sentences. Use the word *up* as an adverb in one and as a preposition in the other.

1. **(adverb)** _____

2. **(preposition)** _____

50 — USING PREPOSITIONAL PHRASES AS ADJECTIVES

When *prepositional phrases* are used to describe, they do the work of *adjectives*.

EXAMPLES: The woman *on the phone* is selling magazines. (Which woman?)
NOUN   ADJ. PHRASE

I wish I had a haircut *like yours*. (What kind of haircut?)
NOUN   ADJ. PHRASE

Underline each prepositional phrase. Then draw an arrow to the noun or pronoun it describes. The first one has been done for you.

1. As the 1900s began, the Arizona territory had trouble <u>with lawbreakers</u>.

2. Gangs of rustlers stole cattle.

3. Bandits with guns robbed ranchers, miners, and travelers.

4. The governor of the territory started the Arizona Rangers.

5. They did a good job with law enforcement.

6. They stopped the frequent fights among miners.

7. Some of the Rangers had once been outlaws themselves.

8. Many people in the territory thanked the Rangers.

9. They called them men of courage.

10. Others thought the band of armed men gave the governor too much power.

B

Add a prepositional phrase to describe each boldfaced noun.

1. The **book** _____ is overdue.

2. The **man** _____ made me angry.

3. His **idea** _____ is foolish.

4. I read a **story** _____.

5. Did you see the **car** _____?

USING PREPOSITIONAL PHRASES AS ADVERBS 51

Some prepositional phrases do the work of *adverbs*. They describe verbs by telling how, when, where, or for how long an action is done.

EXAMPLES: He sang **with great feeling**. (*How* did he sing?)

The concert began **at 8:00 P.M.** (*When* did it begin?)

His family sat **in the first five rows**. (*Where* did they sit?)

The singer performed **for two hours**. (*How long* did he perform?)

 A

Draw an arrow from the boldfaced prepositional phrase to the verb it describes. Decide what question the phrase answers. Write *how, when, where,* or *how long* in the blank.

1. Imagine that you are living **in 1901**. _____

2. Like many Americans, you live **in the country**. _____

3. You cannot easily get **to stores**. _____

4. You shop **by mail-order catalog**. _____

5. **With great interest**, you read every ad. _____

 B

Draw a line under the prepositional phrases and circle the words they describe. Decide whether each phrase is an *adjective* or *adverb* phrase. Then write *adverb* or *adjective* above each phrase. The first one has been done for you.

1. Water (began flowing) *adverb* from the fountain *adverb* in early June.

2. Children of all ages stood under the waterfalls.

3. They played and splashed water on their friends.

4. The hot pavement sizzled on all sides of the fountain.

5. The ground beneath the children's feet was cool and wet.

The word *to* is usually used as a preposition. It can also be part of an *infinitive* (the word *to* plus the plural form of an action verb). Learn to recognize the difference.

EXAMPLES: We went **to the pool**. (PREPOSITIONAL PHRASE)

We wanted **to swim**. (INFINITIVE)

A

Write *P* or *I* to tell whether the boldfaced word group is a *prepositional phrase* or an *infinitive*.

1. _____ Archeologists wanted **to learn** how people once lived.

2. _____ A group of them traveled **to Egypt**.

3. _____ They hoped **to find** ancient tools and artwork.

4. _____ The archeologists dug a tunnel **to a buried tomb**.

5. _____ They used crowbars **to pry** open the heavy door.

6. _____ This chamber had been used **to bury** a king and his belongings.

7. _____ The valuable objects inside were keys **to a past era**.

8. _____ It would now be easier for students **to understand** a lost civilization.

B

Write two original sentences. In the first sentence, use the prepositional phrase "to the farm." (*Farm* will be a noun, the object of the preposition.) In the second sentence, use the infinitive "to farm." (*Farm* will be a verb, part of the infinitive.)

1. _____

2. _____

14. USING PREPOSITIONS CORRECTLY

USAGE NOTES

Remember these hints as you use prepositions in your writing.

- Place prepositional phrases near the words they describe. In the examples below, notice which sentence more clearly tells who has the earache.

    EXAMPLES: We took the baby to the doctor **with an earache**. (MISPLACED PHRASE)

    We took the baby **with an earache** to the doctor. (CORRECTLY PLACED PHRASE)

- Don't use unnecessary prepositions at the end of a sentence.

    EXAMPLES: Where are you going **to**? (INCORRECT)

    Where are you going? (CORRECT)

A

Write *C* or *I* to tell whether each sentence is *correct* or *incorrect*.

1. _____   Can anyone tell me where my umbrella is at?

2. _____   He gave a present to his sister wrapped in bright paper.

3. _____   Where does this old, steam-powered train go?

4. _____   Why did you go to the movies without me for?

5. _____   The girl with the cough is staying home from school.

6. _____   The boy will not attend the wedding with the flu.

B

Rewrite each sentence. Clarify meaning by moving the prepositional phrase closer to the word it describes. The first one has been done for you.

1. A farmer sold a pig in need of money.

    A farmer in need of money sold a pig.

2. In a large, steaming pot she served the spaghetti.

    _____

3. Mr. Lee read us a story about a dogsled race in school today.

    _____

15. DEMON PREPOSITIONS

Be careful when using certain often-confused prepositions.

- **between/among:**

  Between refers to two people, things, or groups.

  EXAMPLE: I must choose **between** the red coat and the black one.

  Among refers to a group of people or things.

  EXAMPLE: I must choose **among** the many coats on the rack.

- **beside/besides:**

  Beside means "next to."

  EXAMPLE: I sit **beside** Clara in history class.

  Besides means "in addition to," or "except."

  EXAMPLES: What subjects will we study **besides** World War II?

  No one **besides** Sue passed the test.

A

Circle the correct proposition.

1. Switzerland is (between / among) two mountain ranges.

2. (Between / Among) Switzerland's four official languages are French and German.

3. (Besides / Beside) making fine chocolates and cheeses, the Swiss are excellent watch-makers.

4. The people of Iceland live (between / among) lava fields, glaciers, and inland lakes.

5. Iceland has little agriculture (beside / besides) grazing land for sheep, horses, and cattle.

6. Nicaragua is a Central American country (between / among) Honduras and Costa Rica.

7. The 300-mile-long Mosquito Coast runs (beside / besides) the Caribbean Sea.

8. Few people live (between / among) the swamps, pine forests, and jungles of the Mosquito Coast.

in/into:

In means "within or inside."

EXAMPLE: The dog is *in* the kennel.

Into means something is moved "from the outside to the inside."

EXAMPLE: I put the dog *into* its kennel.

at/about:

When speaking of time, use *at* to tell the exact time.

EXAMPLE: The movie begins *at* 8:15 P.M.

Use *about* to tell the approximate time.

EXAMPLE: Dinner should be ready *about* 6:00.

┌─ **DID YOU NOTICE?**

It is not correct to say,

"Dinner should be ready *at about* 6:00."

There is no need to use both prepositions (*at* and *about*) to express approximate time.

B

Complete each sentence with *in* or *into*.

1. Are you planning to keep that bug _____ a jar?

2. Make sure to put some leaves _____ the bug house.

3. There is already plenty of salt _____ the soup.

4. Please don't sprinkle any more _____ the pot.

5. I hope you didn't put walnuts _____ this cookie dough.

6. If I eat walnuts, I get bumps _____ my mouth.

7. Five people live _____ this small house.

8. We try not to track mud _____ the rooms.

C

Explain the difference in meaning between these two sentences.

1. We will serve lunch at noon.   2. We will serve lunch about noon.

Sentence #1 means _____

Sentence #2 means _____

A Study the boldfaced words in each column. Then write a letter to show which word or words on the left defines the boldfaced words on the right.

1. _____ **preposition**   a. The story **by** Edgar Allan Poe was scary.

2. _____ **object of preposition** b. The story **by Edgar Allan Poe** was scary.

3. _____ **prepositional phrase**   c. The story by **Edgar Allan Poe** was scary.

B Complete each phrase by adding a preposition from the box. Hint: There may be more than one correct choice for each phrase.

about	after	among	at	before	beside	between
during	in	into	over	on	without	under

1. _____ the morning

2. _____ the ballgame

3. _____ December

4. _____ you and me

5. _____ last night's dinner

6. _____ tomorrow

7. _____ a doubt

8. _____ the package

9. _____ 5:00

10. _____ the hill

11. _____ the suitcase

12. _____ the street

C Underline each *prepositional phrase* and circle the word it describes. Then write *adj.* or *adv.* on the line to tell whether the phrase works as an *adjective* or an *adverb*. The first one has been done for you.

1. _adj._ (Edgar Allan Poe) is among America's most famous writers.

2. _____ Many of his works are mysterious and gloomy.

3. _____ "The Raven" is one of Poe's most famous poems.

4. _____ Critics often compare the writer Steven King with Poe.

5. _____ King also writes tales of mystery and terror.

6. _____ His characters often find themselves in scary situations.

7. _____ It may be best not to read these stories at bedtime!

8. _____ If you get scared, you might stay awake for hours.

D Underline each misplaced prepositional phrase. Then draw an arrow showing where it should appear. Hint: There may be more than one correct place. The first one has been done for you.

1. I took the dog to the veterinarian <u>with fleas</u>.

2. The people could not hear the singer in the last row.

3. I could see the bald eagle with my binoculars.

4. The salesman sold me the car with a convincing speech.

5. I found the letter that my sister had written in an old shoebox.

6. The student could not see the blackboard with the broken glasses.

7. A trophy went to every winner with gold letters.

8. A dessert is not good for people with lots of sugar.

9. In taco shells my sister likes meat, lettuce, and cheese.

10. The clowns teased the party guests with big red noses.

E Write five sentences containing *prepositional phrases*. Then underline each prepositional phrase. You might use some of the phrases from Part B in your sentences.

1. _____

2. _____

3. _____

4. _____

5. _____

CONJUNCTIONS AND INTERJECTIONS

UNIT

7

FOR HELP WITH THIS UNIT, SEE THE REFERENCE GUIDE, RULES 44–48.

 RECOGNIZING CONJUNCTIONS

A *conjunction* is a connecting word. It joins single words, word groups, and sentence parts.

EXAMPLES: Jack *and* Jill went up the hill. (joins single words)
We went over the river *and* through the woods. (joins word groups)
Jack fell down, *and* Jill came tumbling after. (joins sentence parts)

A *coordinating conjunction* connects ideas of equal importance. Commonly used coordinating conjunctions include *and, but, or, yet, for, nor,* and *so.* Coordinating conjunctions can join equal sentence parts to form a *compound sentence.*

EXAMPLES: I love chocolate ice cream, *but* Lily prefers vanilla.

Note that a comma is used before the conjunction to separate the parts of a compound sentence.

Circle each coordinating conjunction.

1. In 1952, King George of England died, and his daughter Elizabeth became queen.

2. She was only 25 years old, yet she ruled a nation.

3. People said their new queen was radiant and lovely.

4. They climbed trees or leaned from windows to see her carriage.

5. The young queen smiled and waved back to the crowd.

B

Fill in each blank with *and, or, but,* or *so.* Hint: More than one choice may be correct.

1. Cars of the 1950s were big, powerful, _____ solid.

2. Their huge tail fins looked great, _____ they didn't add power.

3. Americans loved their cars, _____ they used them more.

4. Drive-in movies _____ restaurants became very popular.

SUBORDINATING CONJUNCTIONS

Subordinating conjunctions connect word groups that are not equal. A subordinating conjunction begins a *subordinate clause*—a group of words that contains a subject and verb but cannot stand alone as a sentence. The subordinating conjunction connects the subordinate clause to a main clause, which can stand alone. The combined clauses form a *complex sentence*.

EXAMPLE:

SUBORDINATE CLAUSE   MAIN CLAUSE

When the bell rang, the students hurried to class.

SUBORDINATING CONJUNCTION

A

Notice punctuation as you circle each subordinating conjunction.

1. Although flat-screen television prices may seem high, they have dropped steadily.

2. While an average flat-screen TV may be an expensive purchase, they were unaffordable only a few years ago.

3. A middle-class family felt lucky if they had one flat-screen TV set.

4. Today some families are not satisfied unless they have a set in every room.

HAVE YOU NOTICED?

A comma appears after a subordinate clause when it is at the beginning of a complex sentence. When the subordinate clause is at the end of the sentence, no comma is used.

B

Choose a subordinating conjunction from the box to fill in each blank. Hint: More than one conjunction may be correct.

after   as   if   because   until   since   unless   when   although   while

1. _____ I cooked dinner, she set the table.

2. The poor dog got sick _____ it ate the spoiled meat.

3. I was late to the party _____ my car had a flat tire.

4. The team will play baseball _____ it rains.

5. _____ Carl practices every day, he is a skilled gymnast.

16. USING COMMAS WITH CONJUNCTIONS

You will not use a comma before every conjunction. Do put a comma before the conjunction in a compound sentence. You will also put a comma after a subordinate clause when it begins the sentence.

A

Use a coordinating conjunction to join two simple sentences. Write the compound sentence on the line, adding the necessary comma. The first one has been done for you.

1. People buy DVD players. They can watch movies at home.

   People buy DVD players, so they can watch movies at home.

2. Families can rent new releases. They can buy DVDs.

   _____

3. VCRs used to be popular. DVD players are easier to use.

   _____

4. I like to rent comedies. I prefer to see adventure films on the big screen.

   _____

B

Join the sentences with a subordinating conjunction. Write the complex sentence on the line. Be sure to add necessary commas.
Hint: **There is more than one correct way to combine each sentence. The first one has been done for you.**

1. Lift weights. You will build muscles.

   If you lift weights, you will build muscles.

2. I do yard work for my neighbors. They pay me well.

   _____

3. Rollerblading is fun. The time seems to fly by.

   _____

4. I can't see the river. There are too many trees.

   _____

Interjections are words and word groups that show feeling. Separate an interjection from the rest of the sentence with a comma. Use an exclamation mark after an interjection that shows excitement.

EXAMPLES: *Oh,* I feel much better now. *Oh!* That is an amazing trick.

A

Underline the interjection in each sentence.

1. Wow! That's Charles Lindbergh.

2. My goodness, this is exciting.

3. Hurry! Let's not miss his take-off!

4. Hurrah! There he goes!

HAVE YOU NOTICED?

When an exclamation mark follows the interjection, the first word in the next sentence is capitalized. When a comma follows the interjection, the next word is *not* capitalized.

B

Rewrite each sentence. Punctuate and capitalize as needed.

1. hurry the British are coming!

_____

2. oh I think I'll skip practice today.

_____

3. my gosh what happened to your hair?

_____

4. yum that was a delicious meal.

_____

C

Write a sentence using each of the following interjections:
stop, oh boy, quick, oops.

1. _____

2. _____

3. _____

4. _____

A Find and underline the *conjunction* or *interjection* in each sentence. Write **C** or **I** above the word to identify its part of speech.

1. After the Civil War, Congress formed the 9th and 10th Cavalries.

2. These were peacetime units, and they included only African-American soldiers.

3. These soldiers protected railroad crews and westward pioneers.

4. Oh, these were indeed some very brave, patriotic men.

5. Was it their strength or their fierce appearance that led the Native Americans to name them the "Buffalo Soldiers"?

6. Wow! Buffalo Soldiers won more than 18 Medals of Honor!

B Circle the conjunction in each sentence. Write **C** or **S** to identify it as a *coordinating* or *subordinating* conjunction. The first one has been done for you.

1. _C_ The Earth has had several ice ages, (and) scientists think the last one began about two million years ago.

2. _____ It began with small sheets of ice, but these sheets steadily grew bigger.

3. _____ When the ice sheets started to move, they picked up huge rocks.

4. _____ The moving rocks scraped and dug at the land.

5. _____ The glaciers slowly melted when the Earth's climate warmed again.

6. _____ They left behind large deposits of dirt and rocks.

7. _____ As the glaciers moved across its surface, the Earth was changed forever.

C Rewrite each sentence, adding an interjection. Remember to include the correct capitalization and punctuation marks.

1. It looks like rain._____

2. Why did you wear that crazy hat? _____

_____

3. I dropped my contact lens! _____

4. You can't eat all of that! _____

5. Have you met my Uncle Ray? _____

6. My tongue is stuck to the freezer door! _____

_____

7. He's getting away. _____

D The following paragraph has too many short sentences. Rewrite the paragraph. Use coordinating and subordinating conjunctions to combine some of the sentences. Remember to use punctuation and capitalization as needed.

I woke up early. Wow! I was surprised! I saw frost on the ground. I saw frost on the trees. It looked like white lace. I knew it was ice. It must have been cold and clear last night. Those are perfect conditions for frost.

_____

_____

_____

_____

_____

SUBJECTS AND PREDICATES
FOR HELP WITH THIS UNIT, SEE THE REFERENCE GUIDE, RULES 49–53.

UNIT

8

56 RECOGNIZING SUBJECTS AND PREDICATES

Remember, every sentence has two main parts. The *complete subject* tells who or what the sentence is about. The part of the complete subject that is a noun or pronoun is the *simple subject*. The *complete predicate* tells something about the subject. The verb in the complete predicate is the *simple predicate*.

EXAMPLE:

COMPLETE SUBJECT | COMPLETE PREDICATE

The *wrestler groaned* loudly.

SIMPLE SUBJECT | SIMPLE PREDICATE

A

Draw a vertical line between the *complete subject* and the *complete predicate*. Then circle the *simple subject* and the *simple predicate*. The first one has been done for you.

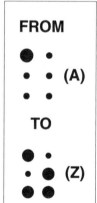

FROM

(A)

TO

(Z)

1. (Louis Braille)(lost) his sight at the age of 3.

2. In school, he became an excellent student.

3. At 15, Braille invented a method of reading for the blind.

4. A pattern of raised dots formed a special alphabet.

5. Blind people could read the dots by touching them.

B

Each sentence is missing either a subject or a predicate. Complete the sentence by adding the needed sentence part.

1. Six sleeping swans _____.

2. Ten tiny toddlers _____.

3. _____ headed for the hills.

4. _____ planted pretty petunias.

17. Avoiding Sentence Errors

A *sentence fragment* is a group of words that is capitalized and punctuated as a sentence but is missing one of the sentence parts.

EXAMPLES: Some very good shows on television. (no predicate)
Plays by the rules in every game. (no subject)

A *run-together* occurs when two sentences are written as one.

EXAMPLES: It isn't a tiger, it's a small cat.
My brother is a real slob his room
looks like a garbage dump.

HAVE YOU NOTICED?

A comma alone cannot link two sentences. Sentences must be separated with a period or joined with a conjunction.

A

Write *S, F,* or *RT* to identify a *sentence, fragment,* or *run-together*.

1. _____ Bob is a busy guy who works part-time on weekends.

2. _____ Bob doesn't have his lawn mower it is at the Johnsons' house.

3. _____ Hard to mow lawns without it!

4. _____ Bob's brother is lazy he never does anything.

5. _____ I often wonder how two brothers can be so different.

B

Add a subject or predicate to each fragment. Rewrite the sentences on the lines.

1. The tiny dog with the biggest ears.

_____

2. Laughing as he ran down the street.

_____

C

Rewrite the run-together sentences as two separate sentences.

1. I love summer vacation gives me free time.

_____

2. I ordered pineapple pizza he refused to eat it.

_____

57 COMPOUND SUBJECTS AND PREDICATES

Two or more subjects may be used with the same predicate. This is a *compound subject*. Two or more predicates may be used with the same subject. This is a *compound predicate*.

EXAMPLES: **Birds** and household **pets** sensed the coming storm.
(compound subject, two main nouns)

He **saw** danger and quickly **called** for help.
(compound predicate, two main verbs)

A

HAVE YOU NOTICED?

Conjunctions join the parts of compound subjects and predicates.

Underline each compound subject or predicate. Then circle the simple subjects and simple predicates. The first one has been done for you.

1. (Rachel Carson) (saw) problems and (wrote) about them.

2. She said the earth and sea were in great danger.

3. Human foolishness and greed had led to pollution.

4. Animals, birds, and fish were dying.

5. Chemical sprays protected plants but killed birds.

B

Write complete sentences by adding a compound subject to each predicate. The first one has been done for you.

1. *A moldy lunch, a denim jacket, and an algebra book* _____ are in my locker.

2. _____
   _____ sit near the back of the room.

3. _____
   _____ keep me busy.

C

Write complete sentences by adding a compound predicate to each subject.

1. A strong earthquake _____
   _____

2. The lifeguard _____
   _____

DIRECT OBJECTS, INDIRECT OBJECTS, AND PREDICATE NOUNS

The predicate of a sentence may include a *direct object*. This is the noun or pronoun that receives the action of an action verb. Remember that the subject of the sentence performs the action. The direct object usually answers the question *What?* or *Whom?*

EXAMPLES: Marco ate the **sandwich**. He enjoyed **it**.

An *indirect object* is the noun or pronoun to whom or for whom an action is done. It comes after the verb and before the direct object. The pronouns *me, you, him, her, it, us,* and *them* are often used as indirect objects.

EXAMPLES: I bought **her** flowers.   I fed the **monkey** peanuts.

A *predicate noun* follows a linking verb and renames the subject.

EXAMPLE: Walter is the **pitcher**.

A

Write DO (direct object), IO (indirect object), or PN (predicate noun) above each boldfaced predicate part. The first one has been done for you.

HELPING HANDS

1. Guide dogs help blind **people**.   *DO*

2. They give **them independence**.

3. Monkeys can be **helpers** too.

4. Trainers have taught **monkeys** to help paralyzed people.

5. Trained monkeys open **doors**, dial **phones**, and turn book **pages**.

6. They serve **people food** and change their television **channels**.

7. Helping Hands is the **organization** that trains these monkeys.

B

Add the missing part to the predicate.

1. This shop repairs _____. **(direct object)**

2. The teacher read _____ a story. **(indirect object)**

3. Today's lunch special is _____. **(predicate noun)**

A Circle a letter to show the correct answer.

1. How many main parts does a sentence have?   a. one   b. two   c. six

2. The main noun in a sentence is called the
    a. compound subject.   b. simple subject.   c. complete subject.

3. The verb is located in the part of the sentence called the
    a. predicate noun.   b. simple predicate.   c. indirect object.

4. A subject that has more than one main noun is called
    a. simple.   b. direct.   c. compound.

B Study the boldfaced sentences. Then write the sentence parts on the lines. The first one has been done for you.

SENTENCE #1: My cousin Sophia followed the ant to its anthill.

1. simple subject: _Sophia_
2. complete subject: _____
3. simple predicate: _____
4. complete predicate: _____
5. direct object: _____

SENTENCE #2: The sturdy little ant was a hard worker.

1. simple subject: _____
2. complete subject: _____
3. predicate noun: _____

SENTENCE #3: The ant brought its children food.

1. simple subject: _____
2. simple predicate: _____
3. direct object: _____
4. indirect object: _____

C Identify each word group by writing **S** *(correct sentence)*, **F** *(fragment)*, or **RT** *(run-together)*. Rewrite the fragments or run-togethers as correct sentences on the lines below.

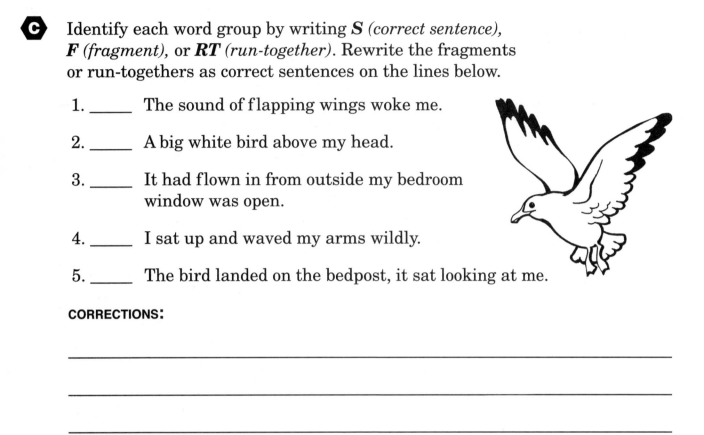

1. _____ The sound of flapping wings woke me.

2. _____ A big white bird above my head.

3. _____ It had flown in from outside my bedroom window was open.

4. _____ I sat up and waved my arms wildly.

5. _____ The bird landed on the bedpost, it sat looking at me.

CORRECTIONS:

_____

_____

_____

D Read the following paragraph. Circle the *main nouns* in the compound subjects. Then underline the *main verbs* in the compound predicates. The first sentence has been done for you.

Clara <u>got</u> a haircut and <u>bought</u> a new sweater for the party. She entered the room. People watched her and whispered. Clara patted her hair and smiled. Cindy and Brad walked toward her. They pointed at something and made strange motions. Were they looking at Clara's hair or admiring her sweater? Cindy spoke softly in Clara's ear and touched the back of her own sweater. Clara turned red and grabbed at her neck. A label and a price tag dangled down the back of the sweater.

PHRASES AND CLAUSES

FOR HELP WITH THIS UNIT, SEE THE REFERENCE GUIDE, RULES 54–58.

UNIT 9

59 RECOGNIZING PHRASES AND CLAUSES

How can you tell if a word group is a *phrase* or a *clause*? The difference is that a clause has a subject and verb, and a phrase does not.

EXAMPLE: **after the first act** (phrase)

after the *students performed* Act I (clause)

SUBJECT   VERB

A

Write *P (phrase)* or *C (clause)* to identify each word group.

1. ____ with a little good luck

2. ____ because the judge was fair

3. ____ while Bob is here

4. ____ before the last bell

5. ____ before the last bell rings

6. ____ in my oldest sister's room

7. ____ where my sister keeps her diary

8. ____ since the puppies were born

9. ____ until the next class meeting

10. ____ until the next class meets

B

Write *phrase* or *clause* above the boldfaced word group. The first one has been done for you.

1. *clause*
   Since we had never been to Arizona, we bought a guide book.

2. **Before the trip** we read articles and studied maps.

3. We read about a place **where the rocks are bright red**.

4. We made plans to visit Arizona **in the spring**.

C

Write two sentences. In the first sentence, use any *phrase* from Part A. In the socond sentence, use any *clause* from Part A.

1. _____

2. _____

Some phrases are used as nouns. They act as the subject of a sentence, an object, or a predicate noun. In Unit 6, you learned that an *infinitive* is made up of the word *to* and the plural form of an action verb. An *infinitive phrase*, which can be used as a noun, begins with an infinitive.

EXAMPLES: Don't try **to guess**. (infinitive used as an object)

   To guess the answers is risky. (infinitive phrase used as a subject)

A *gerund* is a verb that ends in *ing* used as a noun. A *gerund phrase* begins with a gerund.

EXAMPLES: **Laughing** is good for one's health. (gerund)

   Laughing at people's mistakes is rude. (gerund phrase)

⬡**A**

Underline each *infinitive* or *gerund* phrase.
Write *I* or *G* to tell the kind of phrase.

1. _____   Finding free time can be difficult.

2. _____   I love to wear new clothes.

3. _____   Planting a garden is more fun in good weather.

4. _____   One part of the program is learning computer skills.

5. _____   Don't forget to water the tulips.

⬡**B**

Add an *infinitive phrase* to each sentence. The first one has been done for you.

1. Raymond loves to *to dance the tango* _____.

2. I want _____.

3. I hope _____ someday.

⬡**C**

Add a *gerund phrase* to each sentence. The first one has been done for you.

1. *Remembering people's names* _____ is hard for Gracie.

2. _____ is hard for me.

3. I rather be _____ !

61 — APPOSITIVE AND VERB PHRASES

Some phrases act as adjectives. They add information and details about something or someone. An *appositive* is a noun that directly follows another noun or pronoun. It tells more about or renames the first noun. An *appositive phrase* contains an appositive noun.

EXAMPLES:

My neighbor's pet pig, **Mooshie**, is nearsighted. (appositive)
Mooshie, **my neighbor's pet pig**, is nearsighted. (appositive phrase)

A *verb phrase* can also be used as an adjective. A describing verb phrase might begin with a present tense verb ending in *ing*, such as *seeing*. It could also begin with a past tense verb, such as *seen*. These verb phrases give more information about a noun or pronoun.

EXAMPLES: **Seeing the lunar eclipse**, the students gasped in surprise.
An eclipse, **seen only on a cloudless night**, is a rare sight.

A

Combine each pair of sentences by making the second sentence an *appositive phrase*. Remember to set off the phrase with commas. The first one has been done for you.

1. Carrie has a great sense of humor. Carrie is my best friend.
   Carrie, my best friend, has a great sense of humor.

2. Wilson is ugly and fat. Wilson is my brother's bulldog.
   _____

3. Wilson ate our flowers. The flowers were prize-winning roses.
   _____

B

Combine each pair of sentences by rewriting the first sentence as a *verb phrase* used as an adjective. The first one has been done for you.

1. I had worked night and day. I became exhausted.
   Having worked night and day, I became exhausted.

2. The village was pounded by steady rains. The village flooded.
   _____

3. I hear sad music. I begin to cry.
   _____

116

18. AVOIDING DANGLING MODIFIERS

When you use a verb phrase as an adjective, make sure the phrase has something to describe. Always tell your reader *who* or *what* is doing the action.

EXAMPLE: ___*Working*___ in the yard all day, ___*I*___ got a sore back.
              ACTION   WHO DID IT

Notice what happens when a writer forgets the "who did it" part of a sentence.

EXAMPLE: ___*Working*___ in the yard all day, my back got sore.

The verb phrase had no one to describe. This kind of phrase is called a *dangling modifier*.

Alameda de las Pulgas

Avenue of the Fleas? Get me out of here!

A

Put a check (✓) by sentences with a dangling modifier.

1. _____ Having taken Spanish, Mexico's street signs were easy to read.

2. _____ Having watched TV all night, my homework was unfinished.

3. _____ Leaning out the window, I called out to my friends.

4. _____ Playing basketball with my brother, my nose got broken.

5. _____ Wearing clothes by Calvin Cutler, the fashion show began.

6. _____ Barking wildly all night, the new puppy kept us from sleeping.

B

Rewrite the sentences. Correct the dangling modifiers by giving the phrase something or someone to refer to. The first one has been done for you.

1. Having read all the rules, the game was easy to play.

   Having read all the rules, I could easily play the game.

2. Standing on the top floor, the city lights sparkled like diamonds.

   _____

3. Seeing the dirty water, swimming was ruled out.

   _____

Remember that a clause contains both a subject and a verb. An *adjective clause* describes a noun or pronoun. This is called a *dependent clause* because it cannot stand alone as a sentence. An adjective clause usually begins with one of the relative pronouns in the box.

who	whose	which	when	that	where	whom

EXAMPLES: The school only hires teachers **who can speak Spanish**.
Steven, **who can speak Spanish**, is sitting in the first row.

HAVE YOU NOTICED?

Commas set off an adjective clause when the information is *not* necessary to the sentence meaning. No commas are used if the clause is needed. *Try this test:* Read the sentence without the clause. If it still makes sense, set off the clause with commas.

A

Underline each *adjective clause*.

1. Franklin Roosevelt, who became president in 1933, suffered from polio.

2. The disease, which usually attacks children, struck Roosevelt at age 39.

3. He was a man who had the courage to overcome his disability.

4. It was the same courage that helped him lead America during the Great Depression.

5. Roosevelt, who could not easily travel, spoke to Americans over the radio.

6. His speeches, which he called "Fireside Chats," were very popular.

B

Complete each sentence by adding an *adjective clause*. Begin the clause with a *relative pronoun* from the box. The first one has been done for you.

1. Abraham Lincoln was the president *who freed the slaves* .

2. New York is the city _____.

3. Baseball is a sport _____.

4. This assignment, _____, is nearly finished.

NOUN CLAUSES AND ADVERB CLAUSES

In a sentence, a *noun clause* does the work of a noun. It can be used as a subject or an object. It usually answers the question *what* or *who*. A noun clause most often starts with one of the words in the box.

how	that	what	whatever	when	where
which	who	whoever	whose	why	whomever

EXAMPLES: ***Where this road will take us*** is a mystery to me.
I hever found out ***how the story ended***.

An *adverb clause* tells something about the action verb in a sentence. It usually answers the question *when*, *where*, or *how*. A subordinating conjunction often begins an adverb clause. If you need to, review subordinating conjunctions in Unit 7.

EXAMPLE:

ADVERB CLAUSE

After the storm passed, a rainbow appeared.

SUBORDINATING CONJUNCTION

HAVE YOU NOTICED?

A *dependent clause* cannot stand alone as a sentence. It must be joined with an independent clause.

 A

Underline each *noun clause* with one line and each *adverb clause* with two lines.

1. Whatever you decide is fine with me.

2. I can't remember why I tied this string on my finger.

3. The map clearly shows which road leads home.

4. Give the award to whomever most deserves it.

5. When my brother's snake was loose, I hid in my room.

6. Hard work is what gets the job done.

 B

Match a *noun clause* from the second column with a word group in the first column. Draw lines to complete the sentences.

1. The new president will be   a. why the game is canceled.

2. The heavy rain is   b. how to make chili.

3. The cookbook tells   c. whoever gets the most votes.

4. Do you always finish   d. what you begin?

A Each sentence below contains an *appositive phrase* or a *verb phrase* used as an adjective. Underline the phrase and circle the noun or pronoun it describes. Then identify the phrase by writing **AP** or **VP** on the line. The first one has been done for you.

1. _VP_ Looking in the mirror, (she) saw new lines and wrinkles.

2. _____ Edgar, the new school cook, makes great enchiladas.

3. _____ Wearing a helmet and pads, I arrive at my babysitting job.

4. _____ Trapped in a cage, the hairy spider did not seem so scary.

5. _____ Bobo, the trained seal, honked the horn loudly.

B Each sentence contains an *infinitive phrase* or a *gerund phrase*. Underline the phrase. Then identify it by writing **IP** or **GP** on the line.

1. _____ Setting up a tent in the rain is a difficult task.

2. _____ You really need to drive more carefully.

3. _____ He took the lie detector test to prove his innocence.

4. _____ Staying in the sun too long can cause skin problems.

C Provide the sentence part named.

1. **(verb phrase)** _____, Mary lost her wallet.

2. **(infinitive phrase)** It is a bad idea _____.

3. **(appositive phrase)** George Washington _____,
   was born in the state of Virginia.

4. **(gerund phrase)** _____ cannot make a person rich!

D Underline each *dependent clause*. Write **adj., noun,** or **adv.** above the clause to identify the job it does in the sentence. The first one has been done for you.

1. Emily looked at the rock star posters *adj.* <u>that decorated her room</u>.

2. She could not believe what she was seeing.

3. The photos, which showed her favorite rock groups, were *moving*!

4. A sound that was clearly guitar music seemed to fill the room.

5. When Emily heard the music, she began to giggle.

6. Whatever was happening in her room was a lot of fun.

7. Emily blinked her eyes, which were wet with tears of laughter.

8. The rock stars who had seemed so real became flat pictures again.

9. What happened in Emily's room that night is still a mystery.

10. No one knows who or what brought the pictures to life.

E Follow the directions to write each sentence.

1. Use an *appositive phrase* in a sentence about a popular film star.

   _____

2. Use an *adjective clause* in a sentence about a professional athlete.

   _____

3. Use a *gerund phrase* to tell about something you do in your free time.

   _____

4. Use a *noun clause* to predict something about the future.

   _____

GRAMMAR AND USAGE REFERENCE GUIDE

SENTENCES

❶ The Sentence: A Complete Thought

A sentence is a language unit that contains a subject and a predicate and expresses a complete thought. A written sentence begins with a capital letter and ends with a period, a question mark, or an exclamation point.

I have two dozen CD's in my collection.
How many CD's do you have?
Listen to this one!

Some complete sentences have only one word. In sentences such as these, the subject is understood to be *you*.

Stop. Help!

❷ Subjects and Predicates

The two main parts of a sentence are the subject and the predicate. The subject names what the sentence is about. It may be a word, a phrase, or a clause.

Dogs are the most loyal pets.
Losing a dog is very sad.

The predicate is the part of the sentence that tells something about the subject. It includes the verb as well as all other words that are not part of the subject.

My brother *is the boy with red hair.*
Is your sister *meeting us in the gym*?

❸ Four Kinds of Sentences

A sentence that makes a statement and ends with a period is called a *declarative sentence.*

The baseball game will go extra innings.

A sentence that asks a question and ends with a question mark is called an *interrogative sentence.*

Which team do you think will win?

A sentence that makes a request or gives a command is called an *imperative sentence.*

Please hand me the popcorn.

A sentence that expresses strong emotion and ends with an exclamation point is called an *exclamatory sentence.*

What an exciting game!

NOUNS

❹ Recognizing Nouns

A noun is the name of a person, place, or thing. A proper noun names a particular person, place, or thing and is always capitalized. All other nouns are common nouns; they are not capitalized.

He climbed the *mountain.*
He climbed *Mount Whitney.*
That *girl* is a scuba diver.
Karen is a scuba diver.

If the proper noun contains more than one word, capitalize all the important words. Do not capitalize a short word such as *of, and,* and *the* unless it is the first word in a title.

Pacific Ocean   The Shining
Dan and Dave's Repair Shop

❺ Abstract and Concrete Nouns

A concrete noun names something that you can see or touch.

boy, Charlie, rock, giraffe, cloud, essay

An abstract noun names a thought, a quality, an idea, or a feeling.

democracy, honesty, delight, theory, pain

❻ Singular and Plural Nouns

Just about every noun has two forms. The singular form names one person, place, or thing.

A *soldier* marched by.
Loyalty is a virtue.

The plural form names more than one person, place, or thing.

The *soldiers* marched by.
His *loyalties* are divided.

❼ Spelling Plural Nouns

Most nouns are made plural by adding *s* to the singular form.

sunflower*s*, oak*s*, porcupine*s*

Nouns that end in *s, ss, ch, sh,* or *x* are made plural by adding *es* to the singular form.

bonus*es*, glass*es*, church*es*, wish*es*, tax*es*

Nouns that end in *y* are made plural in two different ways. If the *y* ending of the singular noun is preceded by a vowel, add *s* to form the plural.

valley / valley*s*   toy / toy*s*

If the *y* ending of the singular noun is preceded by a consonant, change the *y* to *i* and add *es*.

bully / bull*ies*   butterfly / butterfl*ies*

Some nouns that end in *f*, *fe*, or *ff* are made plural by adding *s*. Others are made plural by changing the *f* to *v* and adding *es*.

staff / sta*ffs*   knife / kni*ves*   half / hal*ves*

There are a number of exceptions to these rules. Always check a dictionary to make sure.

Nouns that end in *o* are made plural in two different ways. When a vowel precedes the *o*, the plural is usually formed by adding *s*.
When a consonant precedes the *o*, the plural is usually formed by adding *es*. Check a dictionary to be sure.

studio / studi*os*   potato / potat*oes*

Some nouns are made plural with a change of internal spelling.

child / *children*   woman / *women*   louse / *lice*

A few nouns are the same in both singular and plural form.

deer / *deer*   moose / *moose*

❽ Possessive Nouns

The possessive form of a noun shows ownership or relationship. A singular noun is made possessive by adding an *apostrophe* and an *s*.

**the state*'s* inhabitants
the governor*'s* decision**

The possessive form of a singular noun that ends in *s* is made by adding an apostrophe and an *s* or by adding just an apostrophe.

**Agne*s's* essay
the bos*s's* office
Mr. Brook*s'* desk**

The possessive form of a plural noun that ends in *s* is made by adding just an apostrophe.

the monkey*s'* cages   the student*s'* lockers

❾ Collective Nouns

Collective nouns name groups of people or things. A collective noun that refers to the group as a whole takes a singular verb.

The crowd *was roaring*.   Our team *is playing*.

A collective noun that refers to the individual members of the group takes a plural verb.

**The committee *are discussing* their differences.
The jury *were arguing* among themselves.**

❿ Compound Nouns

A compound noun combines two or more words into one. Some compound nouns contain hyphens, but most do not.

sunshine, heartbeat, standard-bearer

Most compound nouns are made plural in the usual ways.

toothbrush*es*, spaceship*s*, sales*men*

To make the plural form, add *s* to the noun in a compound that also contains with describing words.

**sergeant-at-arms / sergeant*s*-at-arms
hanger-on / hanger*s*-on**

⓫ Suffixes That Form Nouns

Certain suffixes make nouns of verbs and adjectives. Some of these suffixes are *dom*, *ness*, *er*, *ster*, *y*, *ion*, *ery*, *ant*, and *or*.

**truthful + *ness* = truthfulness
sail + *or* = sailor**

═ PRONOUNS ═

⓬ Recognizing Pronouns

Personal pronouns are words used to replace nouns in sentences. The noun the pronoun replaces is called its antecedent. A pronoun must agree with its antecedent in number (singular or plural) and gender (masculine, feminine, or neuter).

**We enjoyed the *folktale* because *it* was funny.
Since *Rob* moved away, I miss *him* a lot.
Where is *Martha* when I need *her*?**

⓭ Subject and Object Forms of Personal Pronouns

The subject forms of the personal pronouns are *I*, *you*, *he*, *she*, *it*, *we*, and *they*.

I drive.	*You* ride.	*She* walks.
It leaks.	*We* applaud.	*They* smile.

The object forms of the personal pronouns are *me*, *you*, *him*, *her*, *it*, *us*, and *them*.

Tell *me*.	Help *him*.	Thank *her*.
Join *us*.	Hide *it*.	Follow *them*.

⓮ Reflexive Pronouns

A reflexive pronoun refers back to a noun or pronoun in the same sentence. Reflexive pronouns end in *self* or *selves*.

**The dancers looked at *themselves* in the mirror.
Louis must take responsibility for *himself*.**

⑮ Possessive Pronouns

Possessive pronouns show ownership or relationship. The following possessive pronouns are used before nouns in sentences: *my, your, his, her, its, our, their.*

> *my* purse *your* tie *his* idea
> *its* purpose *our* home *their* problem

Possessive pronouns that may not be used before nouns are *mine, yours, his, hers, its, ours, theirs.*

> Is the blue bike *his* or is it *hers*?
> The tan house is *theirs*. *Ours* is next door.

Notice that possessive pronouns, unlike possessive nouns, do *not* include an apostrophe.

⑯ Demonstrative Pronouns

Demonstrative pronouns point out persons, places, and things. *This, that, these,* and *those* are demonstrative pronouns. *This* and *these* point out things that are nearby. *That* and *those* indicate things that are farther away.

> *These* are my clothes. *Those* are falling stars.

⑰ Relative Pronouns

Relative pronouns connect a noun or another pronoun with a word group that tells more about it. The relative pronouns are *who, whom, whose, which,* and *that.*

> Matt had a flat tire, *which* he had to repair.
> The girl *who* lives in Denver represents Colorado.

The relative pronouns *who, whom,* and *whose* refer to people. *Who* is used as a subject, *whom* is used as an object, and *whose* shows ownership or relationship. The relative pronouns *that* and *which* refer to places or things.

⑱ Interrogative Pronouns

Interrogative pronouns are used to ask questions. The interrogative pronouns are *what, which, who, whom,* and *whose.*

> *Which* singer do you like best?
> To *whom* are you speaking?

⑲ Indefinite Pronouns

Indefinite pronouns stand on their own because there is usually no specific antecedent.

> Is *anybody* here?
> *Something* is missing.
> She explained *nothing.*

VERBS

⑳ Recognizing Verbs

A verb is always part of a sentence's predicate. An action verb expresses physical or mental action.

> Kyle *chopped* wood. Kelly *eats* lunch.

A linking verb expresses what is or seems to be. It links the subject with the predicate.

> Wendy *seems* tired. The debaters *are* ready.

Many linking verbs can also be used as action verbs.

Subject-Verb Agreement

㉑ A verb and its subject must agree in person (I, you, he/she/it), number (singular or plural), and gender (masculine, feminine, or neuter).

> I *am* going (**not:** I *are* going)
> They *play* well. (**not:** They *plays* well.)
> Carlos broke *his* wrist.
> (**not:** Carlos broke *her* wrist.)

Some nouns are plural in form, but singular in meaning. Use singular verbs with these words.

> Athletics *is* his interest.
> (**not:** Athletics *are* his interest.)

The words *one, each, every, neither, either, everyone, nobody, everybody,* and *somebody* always take a singular verb.

> Everyone *is* invited. (**not:** Everyone *are* invited.)

Compound subjects joined by and are usually plural. They take a plural verb form.

> Dogs and cats *fight.* (**not:** Dogs and cats *fights.*)

Compound subjects joined by or are usually singular. They take a singular verb form.

> Chocolate or vanilla *is* fine with me.
> (**not:** Chocolate or vanilla *are* fine with me.)

Verb Tense

㉒ A verb's tense shows when it is happening in time (past, present, or future). Verbs change form to show changes in time. The ending *d* or *ed* is usually added to a verb to show past tense. The helping verbs *will* and *shall* are used to express future tense.

> Teresa *works.*
> Teresa *worked.*
> Teresa *will work.*

Verbs that change tense in this predictable way are called regular verbs.

㉓ Irregular Past Tense Verbs

Irregular verbs do not form the past tense with the addition of *d* or *ed*. Instead, they change internal spelling.

grow/*grew*   run/*ran*   tell/*told*   see/*saw*

㉔ Verb Phrases

A verb phrase is made up of two or more verbs that function together in a sentence. The last verb in a verb phrase is the main verb.

We *have enrolled*.   The car *had vanished*.

In a verb phrase, the *ing* ending is used to show continuing action in the present.

They are *voting*.   Mr. Crenshaw is *teaching*.

Action in the past is usually shown by adding *d*, *ed*, *n*, or *en* to the plural form of the main verb. The main verb usually follows a form of the helping verb *have*.

Finally, he *had told* his mother.
He *had dreaded* upsetting her.

A form of the word *do* is often used as a helping verb in a verb phrase.

Why *did* you *scream* like that?
Do you *have* no self-control?

The helping verbs *can*, *could*, *may*, *might*, *must*, *should*, and *would* are often used in verb phrases.

Could you *drive*?   I *might join* you.
Must you *leave* early?   I *can stay* later.

㉕ Active and Passive Verb Phrases

In sentences written in the active voice, the subject *performs* the action. In sentences written in the passive voice, the subject *receives* the action. To write in the passive voice, use a form of the helping verb *be* and a past tense verb.

The package *was shipped*.
The actors *were applauded*.

Usually, the passive voice should only be used when the writer doesn't know who or what performed the action. Most good writing is in the active voice.

═ ADJECTIVES AND ADVERBS ═

㉖ Recognizing Adjectives

An adjective is a word that describes a noun or pronoun. An adjective usually appears *before* a noun or *after* a linking verb.

Adjectives usually tell *what kind*, *which one*, or *how many*.

Clever jokes make me laugh.
Elaine's jokes are *hilarious*.

Adjectives that tell *which one* or *how many* always come before nouns.

Several students got *perfect* scores.
That student didn't take *this* test.

Adjectives that tell *what kind* can sometimes stand alone.

George felt *discouraged*.
Holly was *delighted*.

㉗ Articles

The words *a*, *an*, and *the* are special adjectives called articles. They come before nouns in sentences. Use *a* before a word that begins with a consonant. Use *an* before a word that begins with a vowel.

a diploma, *a* school, *an* idea, *an* interview

Use *a* and *an* with singular nouns. *The* is used with both singular and plural nouns.

a bird / *the* birds   *an* elephant / *the* elephants

㉘ Predicate Adjectives

Predicate adjectives often appear after linking verbs. They tell more about the subject noun or pronoun.

The baby *was premature*. His health *is poor*.

㉙ Proper Adjectives

A proper adjective is an adjective formed from a proper noun.

the Denver Mint, Chinese food,
the Victorian era

㉚ Using Adjectives to Compare

Adjectives can be used to compare two or more people or things. The comparative form is used to compare two people or things. To make the comparative form, add *er* to one-syllable adjectives and most two-syllable adjectives.

a great interest / a *greater* interest
a friendly neighbor / a *friendlier* neighbor

Use *more* or *less* before some two-syllable adjectives and before all adjectives with more than two syllables. Check a dictionary if you're not certain of the correct comparative form.

fearful / *more fearful*   desirable / *less desirable*

The superlative form of an adjective is used when more than two people or things are compared. Add *est* to adjectives with one syllable and to many adjectives with two syllables.

smart/smarter/*smartest*   ugly/uglier/*ugliest*

To make the superlative form, use *most* or *least* before some two-syllable adjectives and all adjectives with more than two syllables. Check a dictionary if you're not certain of the correct superlative form.

beautiful/more beautiful/*most beautiful*
intelligent/ less intelligent / *least* intelligent

㉛ Irregular Adjective Forms

The comparative and superlative forms of *good*, *bad*, *many*, and *much* are irregular. Study the forms shown in the examples.

the good news/the *better news*/the *best news*
a bad result/a *worse result*/ the *worst result*
many chances/ *more chances*/*most chances*
much damage/ *more damage*/*most damage*

㉜ Recognizing Adverbs

An adverb is used to describe a verb, an adjective, or another adverb. Adverbs tell *how*, *when*, *where*, or *how often*.

They arrived *early*.
The hall filled *quickly*.
We drove *downtown*.
The paper is delivered *daily*.

㉝ Adverb Placement

Adverbs that describe verbs can often be placed before or after the verb without changing the sentence's meaning. Adverbs that describe adjectives and adverbs usually are placed before the words they describe.

He ate *noisily*.
He *noisily* ate.
It is *uncomfortably* hot.

㉞ Comparative and Superlative Forms of Adverbs

When no more than two people or things are compared, use the comparative form of the adverb. This form is made by adding *er* to some short adverbs and by adding *more* or *less* before most adverbs.

She jumps *higher* than I do.
I got up *earlier* than you did.
Lou is *more studious* than Sue.
Sue is *less ambitious* than Lou.

Use the superlative form of an adverb to compare more than two people or things. This form is made by adding *est* to some short adverbs. Use *most* or *least* before most adverbs.

The *latest* date to apply is July 1.
Maya is the *most curious* girl I know.
Neil is the *least courageous* lion tamer.

㉟ Negative Adverbs

Negative adverbs, like *not* and *never*, cancel the action of the verb or deny the state of being. Other negatives are *no*, *no one*, *nobody*, *nothing*, *nowhere*, *none*, *hardly*, *barely*, and *scarcely*.

You will *not believe* my story.
I would *never lie* to you, however.

㊱ Avoiding Double Negatives

Use only one negative word in a sentence.

I had *no* lunch.
I had *nothing* for lunch.
I did *not* have anything for lunch.

=== PREPOSITIONS ===

㊲ Recognizing Prepositions

A preposition shows the relationship between a noun and other words in a sentence. Some common prepositions are *on*, *in*, *under*, *before*, *behind*, *with*, *without*, *toward*, *over*, and *through*.

on the wall   *over* the bridge   *up* the chimney

㊳ Prepositional Phrases

A preposition is always part of a word group called a prepositional phrase. A prepositional phrase begins with the preposition and ends with a noun or pronoun.

upon the shelf   in the house   along the river

㊴ The Object of the Preposition

The noun or pronoun that follows a preposition is its object.

We gave a party for *Jared*.
I hide money beneath my *bed*.

㊵ Personal Pronouns in Prepositional Phrases

A personal pronoun in a prepositional phrase is in the object form. The object forms of personal pronouns are *me*, *you*, *him*, *her*, *it*, *us*, and *them*. Notice that when the object of a preposition is a pronoun, the prepositional phrase usually has only two words.

I borrowed a pen *from him* and loaned it *to her*.

41 Using Prepositional Phrases as Adjectives

When prepositional phrases describe nouns or pronouns, they do the work of adjectives.

Bushels *of apples* filled the truck.
Most students *in our class* buy lunch.

42 Using Prepositional Phrases as Adverbs

When prepositional phrases describe verbs, adjectives, or adverbs, they do the work of adverbs.

In 1920, radio was a high-tech invention.
Do you live *within walking distance* of school?

43 Prepositional Phrases and Infinitives

The word to is sometimes used as part of the infinitive verb form rather than as a preposition. The infinitive form contains the word *to* and the plural form of an action verb.

To jump that high is truly amazing.

=== **CONJUNCTIONS AND INTERJECTIONS** ===

44 Recognizing Conjunctions

A conjunction is a connecting word. Conjunctions are used to join single words, word groups, and sentence parts. The most common conjunctions are *and*, *but*, *or*, *nor*, *because*, *although*, *so*, *unless*, and *until*.

I had to wait, *so* I read my book.
Bananas *and* grapes are my favorite fruits.
Jake will leave, *unless* you ask him to stay.

45 Subordinating Conjunctions

Subordinating conjunctions connect word groups that are not equal. This kind of conjunction begins a subordinate clause, a group of words that contains a subject and a verb but cannot stand alone as a sentence. When a subordinate clause is joined to a main clause, which can stand alone, a complex sentence is formed.

Subordinate clauses are adverb clauses. They tell *when*, *where*, *how*, or *why*.

Mia runs to her baby *whenever he cries.*
Before I fall asleep, I always say my prayers.

Commas with Subordinating Conjunctions

46 Use a comma after a subordinating clause that begins a sentence.

Because of bad weather, the concert was canceled.

47 Coordinating Conjunctions

A coordinating conjunction joins two equal parts of a sentence. The most common coordinating conjunctions are *and*, *but*, and *or*.

Heather is an actress, *and* her brother is her manager.
Kevin Callahan *or* Mike Perez will raise the flag.
Joe likes skateboarding, *but* he likes ice skating better.

48 Recognizing Interjections

Interjections are words that express emotion or feeling. A comma separates a mild interjection from the rest of the sentence. An exclamation point is used after an interjection that shows greater excitement.

Oh, it's only you.   *Oh, no!* My car's on fire!

=== **SUBJECTS AND PREDICATES** ===

49 Simple and Complete Subjects

The simple subject in a sentence is its most important noun or pronoun. The object of a preposition cannot be the sentence's simple subject.

The best *sprinter* on the track team is Henry.
A 12-year-old *girl* rescued the drowning swimmer.

A complete subject includes the simple subject and all other words that are not part of the predicate.

Going to school without breakfast is foolish.

Simple and Complete Predicates

50 The simple predicate in a sentence is the verb or verb phrase.

Golfer Gary Player *has* always *had* many fans.
His admirers *follow* him from hole to hole.

A complete predicate includes the simple predicate and all other words that are not part of the subject.

Merton *believes that regular exercise is essential.*

Compound Subjects and Predicates

51 A compound subject is a combination of two or more subjects used with the same predicate.

Tetras and angelfish are two of my favorites.

A compound predicate is a combination of two or more predicates used with the same subject.

Watch them *swim to the surface and gobble their food.*

52 Direct Objects, Indirect Objects, and Predicate Nouns

A direct object is the noun or pronoun that receives the action of the verb.

Jason hit the *ball*. He dropped the *bat* and ran.

An indirect object is the noun or pronoun for whom an action is done.

Shawn gave *me* his coat.

A predicate noun follows a linking verb and renames the subject.

Frederick P. Lawton is the *mayor* of our town.

53 Sentence Fragments and Run-Togethers

A sentence fragment is a group of words capitalized and punctuated as a sentence but lacking an important sentence part.

The child in the blue jacket.
Right after the earthquake.

A run-together is a combination of two sentences incorrectly punctuated as one.

Marcy doesn't like drawing she'd rather paint.

═══ **PHRASES AND CLAUSES** ═══

54 Recognizing Phrases and Clauses

A clause is a group of words that has a subject and a verb.

until the votes are counted
when the campaign continues

A phrase is a group of words that lacks a subject or a verb.

while voting   since Easter Sunday

55 Infinitive and Gerund Phrases

An infinitive phrase can be used as a noun. It begins with an infinitive (the word to followed by the plural form of an action verb).

To swim in that creek could be dangerous.
The sweaty children wanted *to cool off*.

A gerund phrase can also be used as a noun. It begins with a gerund (a verb that ends in *ing* and is used as a noun).

Fishing for bass is lots of fun.
We don't mind *releasing the fish* we catch.

56 Phrases Used to Describe

Phrases that function as adjectives tell more about nouns or pronouns. An appositive is a noun or noun phrase that directly follows and explains another noun.

Brenda, *my cousin from New York*, is visiting.
Our senator, *Helen Bradley*, is out of town.

A verb phrase can also function as an adjective. It may begin with a present tense verb ending in *ing*. It might also begin with a past tense verb, such as *seen*.

Waiting for orders, the soldiers stood at attention.

57 Dependent and Independent Clauses

A dependent clause may function as a noun, an adjective, or an adverb within a sentence. It *cannot* stand alone.

After the tornado was over, rescue workers arrived.

An independent, or main, clause can stand alone as a sentence.

The tornado was over.

58 Clauses Used to Describe

An adjective clause, which usually begins with a relative pronoun, describes a noun or a pronoun. The relative pronouns are *who, whose, which, when, that, where,* and *whom.*

Players *who have come to all practices* will make the trip.

Noun clauses can be used as subjects or objects. They usually begin with *who, whose, whoever, why, whomever, which, how, that, what, whatever, when,* and *where.*

Whatever you need will be provided.
Bill can't understand *why Lorna cried.*

An adverb clause tells more about the action verb in a sentence. An adverb clause often begins with a subordinating conjunction. It answers the question *when, where,* or *how.*

Come to my house *before school starts.*

ENGLISH IN CONTEXT

■ PROGRAM DESCRIPTION

Mastery of basic language skills is the overarching goal of the *English in Context* **series.** To this end, each of the six worktexts has been carefully designed to "begin at the beginning" and gradually proceed along the skills continuum. The low reading level (approximately 4.0) is consistent throughout the program.

The worktexts are appropriate for use with small groups, a full class, or by independent learners. The self-explanatory nature of the lessons frees the teacher for individual mentoring. Students from middle school through adult classes will appreciate the variety of contextual themes, which include humor, amazing facts, historical highlights, and excerpts from real-world documents and forms, as well as high-interest material from academic content areas.

Both illustrations and graphic art are used to support the instruction and maintain interest. A variety of puzzles, riddles, and games are intended to sharpen critical thinking skills as they provide additional interest and amusement. A handy reference guide at the back of each worktext promotes the invaluable habit of "looking up" a verifying reference when usage is in doubt.

■ TEACHING THE PROGRAM

◆ Make sure that *every* student has a dictionary close at hand. Many lessons refer the student to a dictionary for the purpose of checking spelling, different forms of the word, synonyms, etc.

◆ Before passing out the worktexts for the first time, anticipate the negative attitudes of students who have experienced little success in previous English studies. Point out that all lessons are short and that examples provided can be used as models. Ask students to read the worktext Introduction aloud, and then follow up with a class discussion. Encourage students to *expect success*. For the first few lessons in a worktext, ask a student volunteer to read the directions aloud while you observe the other students, making certain that the instructions are understood.

◆ Lesson extensions for homework and/or extra credit might include locating examples of "English in context" in newspaper or magazine clippings, or creative writing assignments such as making posters or charts, writing song lyrics or product descriptions, or finding and recording examples of the focus skill from their basal textbooks. *Realia* (actual business letters, operating instructions, classified ads, etc.) are extremely effective for demonstrating the relevance and everyday application of basic English skills.

◆ Challenge students to find errors in written materials from the "real world." Offer bonus grade points for examples of missing commas, incorrect capitalization, grammar slip-ups, etc.

◆ Riffle through each student's worktext on a regular basis, checking to see that all assigned lessons are completed. If you think it useful, conduct a short weekly "answer-checking" session with the entire group. Keep an eye out for students who aren't making progress. Record unit review scores on the class record chart provided.

◆ Students who are unable to keep pace with their classmates need individual evaluation. Those having difficulty with the reading level could be assigned a peer tutor or perhaps work together in a small group to thoroughly preview and follow up on lessons that are causing them problems. Some ESL students need more oral language practice before transitioning into an entire lesson presentation in print. *All* students need continuing encouragement from the teacher as well as his or her unflagging expectation of success.

◆ As students proceed through the worktexts, periodically reinforce selected skills and subskills in one of the following ways:

(1) Choose an entry from the reference guide, write it on the board, and ask students to supply examples.

(2) Integrate basic English skills instruction in various content-area presentations by asking questions about grammatical structure, interesting vocabulary, "rule-breaker" spellings, or any exemplary written formats.

(3) Reinforce the correlation between spoken and written language by eliciting oral responses to the types of questions asked in the worktext lessons, e.g., "Can anyone name the part of speech for each word in the chapter title?"

◆ CLASS RECORD CHART

Record the number of items missed on each Unit Review next to the student's name. If there are more than two errors, remediate as necessary.

ENGLISH IN CONTEXT

GRAMMAR AND USAGE

STUDENTS	UNIT 1	UNIT 2	UNIT 3	UNIT 4	UNIT 5	UNIT 6	UNIT 7	UNIT 8	UNIT 9
1.									
2.									
3.									
4.									
5.									
6.									
7.									
8.									
9.									
10.									
11.									
12.									
13.									
14.									
15.									
16.									
17.									
18.									
19.									
20.									
21.									
22.									
23.									
24.									
25.									
26.									
27.									
28.									
29.									
30.									
31.									
32.									
33.									
34.									
35.									

ANSWER KEY

1 SENTENCES

1. The Sentence: A Complete Thought
A. 1. S 2. NP 3. NS 4. S 5. S 6. NS 7. S
B., C. Answers will vary.

2. Subjects and Predicates
A. 1. <u>The basketball star</u> sells shoes.
2. <u>I</u> see him on television.
3. <u>He</u> wears Marvelo Star-Jumpers.
4. <u>The shoes</u> are red and gold.
5. <u>He</u> can jump very high.
6. Maybe <u>I</u> should buy the shoes.

B. Answers will vary.

C. 1. I <u>love the commercial with the talking dog</u>.
2. He <u>tells about Crispo Chips</u>.
3. Real dogs <u>can't talk</u>.
4. Crispo Chips <u>taste terrible</u>.
5. Most people <u>won't like the chips</u>.
6. They <u>will like the ad much better</u>.

D. Answers will vary.

3. Four Kinds of Sentences
A. 1. e 2. d 3. a 4. b 5. c 6. f
B. 1. Weather forecasters noticed a warm ocean current**.**
2. **T**hey called the strange effect El Niño.
3. Heavy winter rains **fell** in California.
4. Tornadoes **hit** in Florida.
5. **El Niño a**ffects **the** climate around the world.

C. 1. INT 2. E 3. D 4. INT 5. D 6. IMP
D. Answers will vary.

1 UNIT REVIEW
A. 1. b 2. d 3. e 4. c 5. a
B. 1. INT 2. D 3. D 4. NS 5. IMP 6. E
C. Answers will vary.

2 NOUNS

4. Recognizing Nouns
A. 1. thing 2. thing 3. thing
4. place 5. thing 6. person
7. person 8. thing

B. Most **people** have heard the **saying,** "as strong as an **oak**." Why is that **tree** such a **symbol** of **sturdiness** and **strength**? One **reason** might be that the **oak** lives a very long **time**—often two or three hundred **years**. The **oak** is also very large. This **giant** sometimes grows to a **height** of 150 **feet** and may have a **trunk** eight **feet** thick.

C., D. Answers will vary.

5. Abstract and Concrete Nouns
A. 1. concrete 2. abstract 3. concrete
4. abstract 5. concrete 6. concrete
7. abstract 8. concrete

B. (friendship) umbrella (loyalty) (patriotism) kitchen (ambition) (truth) (health) workman student
1., 2., 3., 4. Answers will vary.

6. Common and Proper Nouns
A. 1. proper 2. common 3. proper
4. common 5. proper 6. common
7. proper 8. common

B. 1. Westhaven Hawks 2. Montclair Junior High 3. History 101
4. Mr. Hall and Ms. Arnett
5. *Romeo and Juliet*

C. Answers will vary.

USAGE NOTES: 1. Capitalizing Proper Nouns
A. 1. **W**est **S**eattle **H**igh **S**chool
2. **C**astle **R**ock **S**tate **P**ark
3. **U**nited **S**tates of **A**merica
4. **R**epublic of **C**hina
5. **L**incoln **S**treet
6. *The Revenge of the Nerds*
7. *A Tale of Two Cities*

B. Answers will vary.

USAGE NOTES: 2. Capitalization Demons
1. aunt, south
2. governor, Pacific Northwest
3. east 4. cousin, East
5. great-uncle, West
6. Professor, dean, college

7. Singular and Plural Nouns

A. 2. details 3. players 4. captains
5. leashes 6. bosses

B. 1. Aphids are tiny insects that often live on branches.
2. Some ants depend on aphids for their meals.
3. An ant will not eat an aphid.
4. Instead, the ant will protect and feed its companion.
5. The aphids product liquid droplets that the ants eat.
6. An old saying says, "Don't bite the hand that feeds you."
7. The ants seem to understand this idea.

C. 1. prizes 2. boxes 3. inches
4. creatures 5. bonuses 6. theaters

8. Plurals: Nouns That End in *y*

A. 1. Marys 2. delays 3. Center Citys
4. flies 5. joys 6. monkeys 7. liberties
8. daisies 9. Jazz Alleys 10. centuries

B. 1. ...mysteries... 2. ...keys...
3. ...loyalties... 4. ...days...

9. Plurals: Nouns That End in *f, fe, ff,* or *o*

A. 1. loaves 2. tomatoes 3. heroes
4. Oreos 5. knives 6. puffs

B. 1. ...buffaloes... 2. ...kangaroos...
3. ...thieves... 4. ...cliffs...

10. Plurals: Unusual Nouns

A. Circle 1, 2, 3, 4, 6, 9, 10, 11, 12

B. ACROSS: 1. gentlemen 3. feet 5. children
DOWN: 1. geese 2. teeth 4. oxen 6. lice

11. Possessive Nouns

A. The planet Mercury would be an uncomfortable place to live. The planet's daytime heat can melt lead. Mercury's nights, however, are very cold. In 1974, America's Mariner 10 passed close to Mercury. Like other space probes, this craft's equipment included cameras. Many photographs were sent back to Earth.

B. 1. Alex's 2. sister's 3. giraffe's
4. worker's 5. neighbor's 6. Sunday's

C. Answers will vary.

12. Plural Possessives

A. 1. S 2. S 3. P 4. P 5. P 6. S

B. party's, King Arthur's, King's, sword's, friends', guests', boy's, girls', era's

13. Collective Nouns

A. 2. team 3. audience

B. 1. P 2. S 3. P 4. S 5. P

14. Compound Nouns

A. 1. doorbells 2. grapefruits
3. toothbrushes 4. maids-of-honor

B. 1. great-uncles 2. raincoats
3. grandchildren 4. sisters-in-law

C. 2. d 3. a 4. b 5. c

15. Suffixes That Form Nouns

A. 2. kindness 3. follower 4. amusement
5. protector or protectant 6. assistant
7. freedom 8. cruelty 9. greenery
10. director 11. youngster 12. plumber

B. 2. pavement 3. improvement
4. stubbornness 5. pigheadedness

USAGE NOTES: 3. Commonly Confused Nouns

A. 1. conscious 2. breath 3. personnel
4. lose 5. conscience 6. loss
7. advice

B. Answers will vary.

② —— UNIT REVIEW ——

A. person, place, or thing

B. 1. confusion 2. roof 3. dog
4. Officer Buckley 5. employer
6. gyms 7. Bill's 8. orchestra
9. wheelbarrow

C. 1. bride's 2. bridesmaids
3. bridegroom's 4. Meg Miller
5. guests' 6. orchestra

D. 1. sandwiches 2. People 3. pubs
4. slices 5. combinations 6. chefs
7. knives

E. 1. Today's 2. Abe McCall's
3. governor's 4. cities' 5. children's
6. students'

3   PRONOUNS

16. Recognizing Pronouns

A. 2. The people … They …
3. The kicker … He …
4. … game … it!
5. …Bobcats …, they …

B. 2. she 3. they 4. he 5. it 6. it

C. 1. They 2. it 3. They 4. He 5. It

D. The telephone = *it*
Alexander Graham Bell = *He*
people = *they*

17. Pronouns as Subjects

A. 1. a 2. b 3. b 4. b 5. a

B. *It* is similar to lawn bowling. *They* played the game. Even today *they* play bocce. *He* is a bocce champ. *It* is not only for me. *She* is the best female player I've seen.

18. Pronouns After Linking Verbs

A. 1. I 2. I 3. we 4. I 5. he

B. 1. he 2. she 3. she 4. he 5. we

19. Pronouns as Objects

A. 1. them 2. me 3. her 4. me
5. me 6. them 7. me

B. 1. us 2. me 3. him 4. her

20. Reflexive Pronouns

A. 2. …mess," *Eric* said. "I … myself."
3. "Well, this old *car* … itself," …
4. "If *we* …ourselves, …
5. Eric's *mother* … herself

B. 1. myself 2. yourself 3. myself
4. herself 5. themselves

21. Possessive Pronouns

A. 1. My 2. our 3. theirs 4. Its 5. your

B. 1. mine 2. my 3. theirs
4. Their 5. their 6. our

USAGE NOTES: 4. Commonly Confused Pronouns

A. 2. it's=*its* 3. who's=*whose*
4. they're=*their*

B. Answers will vary.

22. Demonstrative Pronouns

A. 1. S 2. S 3. P 4. S 5. P

B. 1. that 2. Those 3. that
4. these 5. that

23. Relative Pronouns

A. 1. He is a *man* whose …
2. Do you know the *kids* who …
3. They say it's the early *bird* that …
4. The *novel* Sounder, which …
5. The *person* whom …

B. 1. who 2. that 3. whom 4. whose

24. Interrogative Pronouns

A. 1. What happened … to whom …?
2. Who …? 3. Which …?
4. For whom …? 5. Which is …, and whose is it?

B. 1. Who 2. whom 3. What
4. Which 5. Whose

25. Indefinite Pronouns

A. 1. No one 2. none 3. Many
4. none 5. Nothing

B. No one knows who murdered Miss Scarlet. Some say it was Colonel Mustard. Everyone saw him in the study with her. Some say he had a knife in his back pocket. All agree that something must be done. Most feel the police should be called.

USAGE NOTES: 5. Using Pronouns Correctly

A. 1. C 2. I 3. I 4. I 5. C

B. 1. … either (name) or *I* …
2. (Name) and *I* …
3. … frightened both (name) and *me*.

C. 1. Whom 2. Who 3. ourselves 4. Whom
5. themselves 6. whom 7. who, himself

D. Answers will vary.

3   UNIT REVIEW

A. 1. d 2. a 3. c 4. e 5. b

B. 1. The name … and its people.
2. Many believe it was ….
3. They once stamped ….
4. People who … said that …."

5. These people said ….
6. Over time, … to like him.
7. His name lost its … for our country.

C. 1. Whose 2. who 3. She, that
4. she, who 5. I, that 6. I, her

D. 1. He 2. whom 3. himself 4. his, me
5. themselves 6. them 7. They, which

E. Answers will vary.

4   VERBS

26. Recognizing Verbs

A. 1. was 2. worked 3. had 4. boasted
5. boarded 6. felt 7. was 8. steamed
9. was leaving, heading 10. were

B. 1. were, brought 2. stowed, guarded
3. felt, looked 4. was 5. seemed
6. stayed, tried 7. reached
8. steamed, avoiding
9. traveled, trying 10. went, hit

C., D. Answers will vary.

27. Action Verbs

A. 1. M 2. M 3. P 4. M 5. M
6. P 7. M 8. M 9. P 10. M

B. Answers will vary.

28. Linking Verbs

A. 1. LV: seems 2. LV: is 3. LV: smells
4. AV: smells 5. LV: appears
6. LV: are 7. AV: appears
8. LV: become 9. LV: remains

B. Answers will vary.

29. Subject-Verb Agreement

A. 1. belongs 2. like 3. see
4. sing 5. weave 6. see

B. 1. imagines=*imagine*, lives=*live*
2. enjoys=*enjoy* 3. tours=*tour*
4. waits=*wait*

C. 1. is 2. is 3. are 4. is
5. is 6. Are

D. 2. about dogs *tells*
3. of diamonds *is*
4. including Oregon *welcome*
5. of flowers *makes*
6. as well as the other workers *is*

USAGE NOTES: 6. Subject-Verb Agreement Demons

A. 1. is 2. are 3. is 4. are

B. 2. belong 3. has 4. are 5. eats 6. wants

C. 1. is 2. is 3. is 4. cost 5. are
6. is 7. requires 8. is

D. Answers will vary.

30. Verb Tense

A. 1. present: is 2. present: looks
3. present: spin 4. present: call
5. past: proved 6. past: moved
7. past: rescued 8. future: will
9. future will

B. Answers will vary.

31. Irregular Past Tense Verbs

A. 2. rang = *ring* 3. drove = *drive*
4. fell = *fall* 5. began = *begin*

B. 2. froze 3. see 4. eat 5. ate 6. grew

32. Verb Phrases: Action in the Present and Past

A. 1. is (HV) hoping (MV) 5. was (HV) asking (MV)
2. is (HV) saving (MV) 6. is (HV) asking (MV)
3. was (HV) working (MV) 7. are (HV) willing (MV)
4. is (HV) delivering (MV)

B. 2. are going 3. are staying
4. is working 5. are getting

C. 2. present: are hoping
3. past: has taken
4. present: is trying
5. past: has had
6. past: has practiced
7. present: is dreaming
8. present: is waiting

D. The rain has fallen for 30 days. It has soaked the hillsides. Now the earth is starting to slide. Some homeowners are building concrete walls. Such walls have stopped landslides in the past. Everyone is praying that the walls hold and the sun shines.

HELPING VERB	PRESENT-TENSE MAIN VERB	PAST-TENSE MAIN VERB
has		fallen
has		soaked
is	starting	
are	building	
have		stopped
is	praying	

33. More Verb Phrases

A. I did (not) expect guests. Did (I) invite you? I do (sometimes) forget these things. I am (a bit) surprised by your visit. Folks do (not usually) call on me at midnight.

B. Answers will vary.

C. The painters will arrive tomorrow. They will probably paint the outside walls tan. We must see samples of the trim colors before choosing. We should select a color right away. We might choose navy blue. What color would you choose?

D.

	HELPING VERB	MAIN VERB
1.	will	hear
2.	will	build
3.	might	travel
4.	might	have
5.	can	be
6.	may	be

USAGE NOTES: 7. Passive Verb Phrases

A. 1. AV 2. AV 3. PV 4. AV 5. PV
6. AV 7. PV 8. AV 9. AV

B. Answers will vary.

USAGE NOTES: 8. Shifts in Verb Tense

A. 1. present 2. past 3. present
4. past 5. future

B. It (was) April Fool's Day. Carrie (planned) to trick her friend Rich. She puts a gift-wrapped box in his locker. Rich (found) the box and is excited. He does not see the air holes in the back. Rich (took) the box out of his locker and quickly opens it. Out jumps a big green toad!

C. Answers will vary.

USAGE NOTES: 9. Troublesome Verbs: *lie* and *lay*, *sit* and *set*, *leave* and *let*, *bring* and *take*, *borrow* and *lend*

A. 1. set 2. sit 3. Set
4. set 5. lay 6. Lie

B. Thanksgiving is a time when my family and friends **set** *sit* down together for dinner. Someone cooks a fine meal and **sits** *sets* out their best dishes. I live in Hawaii, and we often **set** *sit* outside for dinner. My Aunt Hannah likes to **lie** *lay* an orchid on each plate. After dinner, I **sit** *set* all the plates on a tray and take them to the kitchen to wash. Some lucky guests just **lay** *lie* around relaxing!

C. 1. Take, Bring—Answers will vary.
2. leave, let—Answers will vary.
3. lend, borrow—Answers will vary.

④ ── **UNIT REVIEW** ──

A. 1. AV pitched 2. LV was 3. AV knew
4. AV put 5. AV reached 6. LV was

B. 1. is 2. protects 3. warns 4. Smell
5. learn 6. acts 7. stops 8. send
9. Think 10. Are 11. feel

C. 2. came—past, singular
3. loved—past, plural
4. play—present, plural
5. knows—present, singular
6. will go—future, plural
7. will buy—future, singular

D. 1. made 2. was 3. saw
4. became 5. earned

E. 1. has (HV) practiced (MV)
2. is (HV) hoping (MV)
3. has (HV) won (MV)
4. is (HV) hosting (MV)

⑤ **ADJECTIVES AND ADVERBS**

34. Recognizing Adjectives

A. 1. messy 2. tidy 3. broken

B. 2. bright, weary 3. dark, fierce 4. foamy, high, wild 5. lonely, young 6. brilliant 7. lost, dense, gray 8. dangerous, shallow 9. sturdy, little

C. Biloxi, Mississippi, is a delightful resort (town). (It) is beautiful and charming. Biloxi sits beside the warm (waters) of the Gulf of Mexico. Neighborhoods of old stucco (cottages) remind visitors of an earlier (era). Huge mossy (oaks) line the brick (streets) there.

D., E. Answers will vary.

35. Articles

A. During (the) Civil War, (the) North and (the) South fought (a) battle in Tupelo, Mississippi. For years Tupelo was (a) busy railroad town. Later it became (the) hometown of (the) "King of Rock and Roll." (The) King was born in (a) small white house. When he grew up he became (a) singer and (an) actor. Do you know (the) name of (the) famous man from Tupelo? Tupelo was (the) birthplace of (the) great Elvis Presley.

B. 1. an 2. a, the 3. the 4. a
5. a, an 6. the, the

36. Adjectives Before Nouns

A. Many people think of (the) Wright brothers as (the) inventors of (the) airplane. In 1902, (these) brothers did successfully fly. But (several) inventors had been dreaming of flight much earlier. In 1842, (an) English inventor, William Samuel Hensen, designed (a) plane powered by steam. About 50 years later, in 1893, Sir Hiram Maxim built (this) type of plane. (The) engine had 300 horsepower. (That) plane crashed in 1894. Sir Hiram was trying to fly in (a) circle above (a) track.

B. 2. *The* (airline) … *the* (bags)
3. *Those* (suitcases)
4. *Each/Every* (piece)
5. *The* (same thing) … *another* (trip)
6. *a* (tag) … *each/every* (bag) I take on *a/any/the* (plane)

37. Adjectives After Linking Verbs

A. 1. The weather is <u>wet</u> and <u>cold.</u>

2. The sky looks <u>dark</u>.

3. The clouds are <u>thick</u>.

4. The fire in …is <u>bright</u> and <u>cheery</u>.

5. It seems <u>inviting</u>.

6. Some hot tea and toast … <u>delicious</u>.

B., C. Answers will vary.

38. Proper Adjectives

A. 1. b 2. a 3. e 4. c 5. d

B. Answers will vary.

C. We drove to Vancouver, British Columbia. After a stop at the (Canadian border), we continued north to the city. There we admired the (Vancouver skyline) of tall buildings and white-capped mountains. We sampled fish from (Canadian) waters and found terrific (Indian, Thai, Italian), and (Chinese) restaurants. Our (Vancouver mornings) began with strolls along the (Stanley Park) walkway. We ended each day watching the sunset at (English) Bay.

39. Possessive Nouns and Pronouns Used as Adjectives

A. 2. … <u>its</u> *paws* … <u>its</u> *surroundings*.

3. <u>Its</u> *hearing* …<u>human's</u> *hearing*.

4. A <u>cat's</u> *eyesight*, ….

5. … <u>their</u> *prey* ….

6. … <u>cat's</u> *eyes* …?

7. The <u>cat's</u> inner *eye* ….

8. … <u>animal's</u> night *vision*.

B. Answers will vary.

40. Using Adjectives to Compare

A. 1. weakest 2. plainer 3. happy
4. darkest 5. cleaner, cleanest

B. Answers will vary.

C. 1. S 2. C 3. S 4. S

D. 1. greatest 2. most valuable
3. biggest 4. more popular

41. Irregular Adjective Forms

A. 1. *best* = superlative
2. *More* = comparative
3. *better* = comparative
4. *worse* = comparative

B. 1. ~~worse~~=*worst* 2. ~~good~~=*better*
3. ~~best~~=*better* 4. ~~worse~~=*worst*

42. Using *Less* and *Least* to Compare

A. 1. least 2. less 3. least 4. less 5. less

B. Answers will vary.

Usage Notes: 10. Spelling Comparative Adjectives

A.

1. dusty	dustier	**dustiest**
2. wet	**wetter**	wettest
3. snowy	**snowier**	**snowiest**
4. angry	**angrier**	**angriest**

B. 1. luckier 2. biggest 3. craziest
4. hotter 5. silliest 6. easier

Usage Notes: 11. Using Specific Adjectives

A. 1. naughty 2. decayed 3. scorching
4. booming 5. drenched 6. polluted
7. ear-splitting 8. muffled 9. crimson
10. towering

B., C. Answers will vary.

43. Recognizing Adverbs

A.

	HOW?	WHEN?	HOW OFTEN?	WHERE?
2.		nightly		
3.			often	
4.	oddly			
5.				underwater
6.	quickly			
7.			usually	
8.			never	
9.			sometimes	

B. 2. … approached … rather cautiously.

3. … flames … extremely hot.

4. …be especially careful.

5. …not want …trapped inside

C. In colonial times, people generously volunteered to fight fires. The strongest volunteers passed very heavy buckets from a well to the fire. Then women and children quickly passed the emptied buckets back to the well. These extremely hard-working townspeople were appropriately called the *bucket brigade.*

D.

ADVERB	WORD DESCRIBED
2. very	heavy (adj.)
3. quickly	passed (verb)
4. back	passed (verb)
5. extremely	hard-working (adj.)
6. appropriately	called (verb)

44. Using Adverbs

A. 1. later 2. yesterday 3. carefully
4. upstairs 5. uncomfortably
6. seldom 7. slightly

B. Answers will vary.

45. Adverb Placement

Wording may vary.
2. The school play clearly was a success. -or- Clearly, the school play was a success.
3. The costumes were brilliantly designed.
4. Sometimes we eat at the Hilltop Cafe. -or- We eat sometimes at the Hilltop Cafe.
5. The food is usually delicious and inexpensive. -or- Usually the food is delicious and inexpensive.
6. Would you like to join me tomorrow for lunch? -or- Tomorrow would you like to join me for lunch?

46. Using Adverbs to Compare

A. 2. C/less swiftly 3. C/better
4. S/fastest 5. C/better
6. C/more fiercely

B. Answers will vary.

Usage Notes: 12. Avoiding Double Negatives

A. 1. ✓ 2. C 3. ✓ 4. C
5. C 6. ✓ 7. ✓

B. Answers will vary.

Usage Notes: 13. Adjective or Adverb?

A. 2. She wore an unusual dress …

3. The hem … uneven.

4. …stared at Lynn curiously.

5. Others were rude … laughed loudly.

6. "Take a good look!" Lynn told them.

7. … had hemmed … unevenly.

8. Lynn is now doing really well …

B. Answers will vary.

UNIT REVIEW

A. MYSTERY WORD=*describe*
1. adjective 2. contraction
3. articles 4. adverb 5. negative

B. 1. F 2. F 3. F 4. T 5. T
6. T 7. T 8. F 9. F 10. T

C. 1. often 2. big, U.S.
3. American, quickly, the
4. cleverly, women's, shorter
5. Short, soon, longer
6. Many, seldom
7. more, practical, wartime, factory

D. 1. well, soft 2. properly, bare
3. really, uncomfortable 4. heavy

E. 1. widest 2. bigger 3. classiest

6 PREPOSITIONS

47. Recognizing Prepositions and Prepositional Phrases

A. 2. … across the street …
3. … in it. 4. For many hours …
5. … against the cold wind.

B. At last, the door of the building swung open with a loud bang. A dark figure moved down the steps toward the bus stop. No one was on the street with the two men except a black cat. The light by the bus stop lit the dark figure's face. "Oops! Wrong man," thought the detective.

C. 1. within 2. to 3. through *-or-* into
4. into 5. over 6. over

D. ACROSS: 2. above 5. except 7. during
9. beside DOWN: 1. behind
3. between 4. near 6. like 8. with

48. The Object of the Preposition

A. 1. … in his room 2. … from the past
3. … with the tunes. 4. … to the Beatles … in a yellow submarine!"
5. … on the bedpost …

B. Answers will vary.

49. Adverb or Preposition?

A. 1. P 2. P 3. P 4. A 5. A 6. P 7. P
8. A 9. A 10. A 11. P 12. P 13. P

B. Answers will vary.

50. Using Prepositional Phrases as Adjectives

A. 2. Gangs of rustlers …
3. Bandits with guns …
4. The governor of the territory …
5. … job with law enforcement.
6. … fights among miners.
7. Some of the Rangers …
8. Many people in the territory …
9. … men of courage.
10. … band of armed men …

B. Answers will vary.

51. Using Prepositional Phrases as Adverbs

A. 1. … living **in 1901**. (when)
2. … live **in the country**. (where)
3. … get **to stores**. (where)
4. … shop **by mail-order catalog**. (how)
5. **With great interest**, you read … (how)

B. 2. Children of all ages *adjective* stood under the waterfalls. *adverb*
3. They played and splashed water on their friends. *adverb*
4. The hot pavement sizzled on all sides *adverb* of the fountain. *adverb*
5. The ground beneath the *adjective* children's feet was cool and wet.

52. Prepositional Phrases or Infinitives?

A. 1. I 2. P 3. I 4. P
5. I 6. I 7. P 8. I

B. Answers will vary.

USAGE NOTES: 14. Using Prepositions Correctly

A. 1. I 2. I 3. C 4. I 5. C 6. I

B. 2. She served the spaghetti *in a large, steaming pot.*
3. Mr. Lee read us a story *in school today* about a dogsled race.

139

USAGE NOTES: **15. Demon Prepositions**

A. 1. between 2. Among 3. Besides
   4. Among 5. besides 6. between
   7. beside 8. among

B. 1. in 2. into 3. in 4. into
   5. in 6. in 7. in 8. into

C. Sentence #1 means *exactly noon.*
   Sentence #2 means *approximately noon.*

⟨6⟩ ——— UNIT REVIEW ———

A. 1. a 2. c 3. b

B. 1. in 2. at 3. during/before/after/ in
   4. about/between 5. about/during/after
   6. after 7. without 8. beside/on/under
   9. about/at/before 10. over/on
   11. beside/in/under
   12. beside/in/into/on

C. 2. adj.—Many of his works are …
   3. adj.—…one of Poe's most … poems.
   4. adv.—compare… with Poe.
   5. adj.—…tales of mystery and terror.
   6. adv.—find… in scary situations.
   7. adv.—read… at bedtime!
   8. adv.—awake for hours.

D. 2. The People could … in … row.
   3. I could …with my binoculars.
   4. The …with a convincing speech.
   5. I found … in an old shoebox.
   6. The Student could … with … glass.
   7. A trophy went …with gold letters.
   8. A dessert is … with lots of sugar.
   9. In taco shells … and cheese.
   10. The clowns teased …with … noses.

E. Answers will vary.

⟨7⟩ CONJUNCTIONS AND INTERJECTIONS

53. Recognizing Conjunctions

A. 1. and 2. yet 3. and 4. or 5. and

B. 1. and 2. but 3. and 4. and

54. Subordinating Conjunctions

A. 1. Although 2. While 3. if 4. unless

B. 1. While 2. because 3. after
   4. unless 5. Because

USAGE NOTES: **16. Using Commas with Conjunctions**

A. 2. … release, *or* they …
   3. … VCRs, *but* other …
   4. … comedies, *but* I prefer …

B. 2. *When* I do yard work for my
   neighbors, they pay me well.
   3. *Since/Because* rollerblading is
   fun, the time seems to fly by.
   4. I can't see the river *because*
   there are too many trees.

55. Interjections

A. 1. Wow 2. My goodness
   3. hurry 4. Hurrah

B. 1. *H*urry*! T*he British …
   2. *O*h*,* I think I'll …
   3. *M*y gosh*! W*hat happened …
   4. *Y*um*! T*hat was a …

C. Answers will vary.

⟨7⟩ ——— UNIT REVIEW ———

A. 1. … 9th <u>and</u> (C) 2. … units, <u>and</u> (C)
   3. … crews <u>and</u> (C) 4. <u>Oh</u>, (I)
   5. … strength <u>or</u> (C) 6. <u>Wow!</u> (I)

B. 2. C 3. S 4. C 5. S 6. C 7. S

C., D. Answers will vary.

⟨8⟩ SUBJECTS AND PREDICATES

56. Recognizing Subjects and Predicates

A. 2. In school, he became an …
   3. At 15, Braille invented a …
   4. A pattern of raised dots formed …
   5. Blind people could read …

B. Answers will vary.

USAGE NOTES: **17. Avoiding Sentence Errors**

A. 1. S 2. RT 3. F 4. RT 5. S

B. Answers will vary.

C. 1. I love summer. Vacation …
   2. I ordered pineapple pizza. He …

57. Compound Subjects and Predicates

A. 2. <u>She said the earth and sea were</u> …
   3. <u>Human foolishness and greed
   had led</u>…
   4. <u>Animals, birds, and fish were dying.</u>
   5. <u>Chemical sprays protected plants
   but killed birds.</u>

B., C. Answers will vary.

58. Direct Objects, Indirect Objects, and Predicate Nouns

A. 2. them (IO), independence (DO)
3. helpers (PN) 4. monkeys (DO)
5. doors (DO), phones (DO), pages (DO)
6. people (IO), food (DO), channels (DO)
7. organization (PN)

B. Answers will vary.

⑧ UNIT REVIEW

A. 1. b 2. b 3. b 4. c

B. SENTENCE #1: 2. My cousin Sophia
3. followed 4. followed the ant to its anthill 5. ant
SENTENCE #2: 1. ant 2. The sturdy little ant 3. worker
SENTENCE #3: 1. ant 2. brought
3. food 4. children

C. 1. S 2. F 3. RT 4. S 5. RT

D. Clara got a haircut and bought a new sweater for the party. She entered the room. People watched her and whispered. Clara patted her hair and smiled. (Cindy) and (Brad) walked toward her. They pointed at something and made strange motions. Were they looking at Clara's hair or admiring her sweater? Cindy spoke softly in Clara's ear and touched the back of her own sweater. Clara turned red and grabbed at her neck. A (label) and a price (tag) dangled down the back of the sweater.

⑨ PHRASES AND CLAUSES

59. Recognizing Phrases and Clauses

A. 1. P 2. C 3. C 4. P 5. C
6. P 7. C 8. C 9. P 10. C

B. 2. phrase 3. clause 4. phrase

60. Infinitive and Gerund Phrases

A. 1. Finding free time (G)
2. to wear new clothes (I)
3. Planting a garden (G)
4. learning computer skills (G)
5. to water the tulips (I)

B., C. Answers will vary.

61. Appositive and Verb Phrases

A. 2. Wilson, *my brother's bulldog,* is ugly and fat.
3. Our flowers, *prize-winning roses,* were eaten by Wilson.

B. 2. *Having been pounded by steady rains,* the village flooded.
3. *Hearing sad music,* I begin to cry.

USAGE NOTES: 18. Avoiding Dangling Modifiers

A. A check (✓) by 1, 2, 4, 5

B. 2. Standing on the top floor, *I could see* the city …
3. Seeing the dirty water, *we ruled out* swimming.

62. Adjective Clauses

A. 1. who became president in 1933
2. which usually attacks children
3. who had the courage … disability
4. that helped … Great Depression
5. who could not easily travel
6. which he called "Fireside Chats,"

B. Answers will vary.

63. Noun Clauses and Adverb Clauses

A. 1. Whatever you decide
2. why I tied this string on my finger
3. which road leads home
4. whomever most deserves it
5. When my brother's snake was loose
6. what gets the job done

B. 1. c 2. a 3. b 4. d

⑨ UNIT REVIEW

A. 2. AP: (Edgar), the new school cook …
3. VP: Wearing a helmet and pads, (I) …
4. VP: Trapped in a cage, … (spider) …
5. AP: (Bobo), the trained seal, …

B. 1. GP: Setting up a tent …
2. IP: … to drive … 3. IP: … to prove …
4. GP: Staying in the sun too long …

C. Answers will vary.

D. 2. adv.: …what she was seeing.
3. adj.: …which … rock groups
4. adj.: … that was clearly guitar music
5. adv.: When Emily heard the music
6. noun: Whatever … in her room
7. adj.: … which were … of laughter
8. adj.: …who had seemed so real
9. noun: What happened … that night
10. noun: … who or what … to life.

E. Answers will vary.